FAMILIES GROWING TOGETHER

FAMILIES GROWING TOGETHER

M. SCOTT MILES

VICTOR BOOKS®

A DIVISION OF SCRIPTURE PRESS PUBLICATIONS INC.
USA CANADA ENGLAND

Library of Congress Cataloging-in-Publication Data

Miles, M. Scott
    Families growing together / by M. Scott Miles
        p.   cm.
    Includes bibliographical references.
    ISBN 0-89693-821-2
    1. Intergenerational Christian education.   I. Title.
  BV1579.M54   1990
268'.6 — dc20   90-37758
                                            CIP

1 2 3 4 5 6 7 8 9 10 Printing/Year 94 93 92 91 90

CONTENTS

INTRODUCTION

My first exposure to intergenerational learning came while I was a student at Fuller Theological Seminary. I enrolled in a family ministries practicum led by Dr. Jim Larson. As part of the course we were required to plan and lead an intergenerational learning experience. Because some of us had no local church affiliation, Jim invited us to participate in a six-week experience he was leading at a nearby Presbyterian church. Six of us chose to participate. What an exciting time we had! Much of what I now practice in intergenerational learning I learned from that experience, both conceptually and logistically.

After graduating from seminary I resolved to continue my journey in intergenerational learning. It seemed to me the benefits that accrued for individual families and a local congregation were well worth the effort. Because I was a youth pastor, my initial focus was on parent-teen experiences. Since then, I have had the opportunity to lead intergenerational learning groups in many settings and with varying types of groups. But the more I became involved in intergenerational learning, the more I heard pastors and people alike expressing the need for such experiences within the church setting. I also noticed a significant lack of curriculum materials on the market for doing intergenerational learning.

After consulting for several pastors who were interested in doing intergenerational learning and providing them with some curriculum helps, I decided to put what I thought I knew down in writing. The result was a curriculum manual consisting of some basic how-to information and several learning units. As I distributed the manual to those requesting assistance, I was encouraged by some to think about possible publication. So, here we are! And I am convinced, now more than ever, that as our world becomes increasingly complex, intergenerational learning will become a more pressing need in the church.

The purpose of this book, then, is to provide the information, format, and resources necessary for a church interested in becoming involved in the exciting ministry of intergenerational-family learning. It is by no means exhaustive. It is basic. It gives some starting points for developing a frame of reference for intergenerational learning, and it provides some units of study to help you get started. Additional resources are listed in the back for your own further study and research.

I am appreciative of the many people who have had a hand in this project coming to fruition. I am grateful to Jim Larson for his willingness to let a green seminarian become involved with him in an intergenerational learning experience. I continue to feel his influence, even as I grow in my own style of leading such experiences.

I am thankful to Jean Book, my secretary when the initial curriculum manual was produced. She typed, retyped, and typed again, drafts of the material without grumbling or complaining.

To the people of Fairview Avenue Brethren In Christ Church, I also say thanks. They cheerfully allowed me the time to work on this project—both in the office, and sometimes out of the office. For their encouragement and support I am deeply grateful. This is especially true of Rev. Lynn Thrush, my senior pastor and partner in ministry.

A special word of appreciation also goes to those of the congregation who agreed to assist me by reviewing and giving input throughout the development of the manuscript—Greg Deardorff, Sally Shearer, Val Dick, and Joyce Leaman. The same word of thanks is also due Dr. John Dettoni, friend, mentor, and professor at Fuller Theological Seminary, who gave valuable input with regard to content and style in the preparation of the manuscript.

I likewise owe a debt of thanks to longtime friend Steve Aldridge, manager of the Logos Bookstore in Champaign, Illinois, for his assistance in researching, locating, and evaluating resources.

But perhaps most importantly, to my wife Judy, who has been my helper, guide, supporter, counselor, critic, and friend these past thirteen years. She continues to expand my horizons of what it means to be a husband, a father, a family, and a pastor. Her highly creative mind and exceptional skills on the computer are quite useful too! This one's for you, Jude.

I sincerely pray that this book will give valuable assistance to those desiring to establish a significant ministry of intergenerational learning in their church. Welcome to the exciting ministry of *Families Growing Together*. Enjoy!

M.S.M.

ONE

Seeing the
Possibilities

"Love the Lord your God with all your heart and with all your soul and with all your strength. These commandments that I give you today are to be upon your hearts. Impress them on your children. Talk about them when you sit at home and when you walk along the road, when you lie down and when you get up. Tie them as symbols on your hands and bind them on your foreheads. Write them on the doorframes of your houses and on your gates" (Deut. 6:5-9).

The Biblical Ideal

The weight of the scriptural evidence leads to one overwhelming conclusion. From the beginning God intended for the home and family to be the seedbed of faith. Parents were to love God. Their love for God was to be shared with their children both formally and informally, verbally and nonverbally. They were to feel so comfortable with their relationship with God that they would discuss it with their children, and with each other, with relative ease. It was to be a normal, natural, spontaneous part of life. Through that lived relationship of faith, children then would come to know the same Lord God and live in a personal relationship with Him.

A beautiful example of Deuteronomy 6 at work is found in the New Testament. In 2 Timothy 1:3-5, the Apostle Paul recalls with affection the great strength of Timothy's faith. But Timothy's faith pointed to a heritage that came from two preceding generations within his own family. His grandmother Lois was a godly woman who imparted her faith to her daughter

Eunice. Eunice, Timothy's mother, imparted that same faith to her son Timothy. Faith in Jesus Christ was an important part of Timothy's family. It was nurtured in the grind of the family's daily routine and passed on from generation to generation.

Another model of the Deuteronomy 6 ideal in action is seen within the early church as a whole. The early church maintained a sense of family wholeness. The faith of the father became that of the child — not through forced indoctrination, but because their faith in Christ was an essential part of their lives together. Parents and children alike met together to participate in the breaking of bread and table fellowship. Mutual sharing and ministry between households was the norm. Children observed the faith commitments of their parents in real, concrete ways. These were shared experiences that took place in the context of home (cf. Acts 2:46-47; 4:32-35; 16:31-34). They were informal experiences woven into the fabric of daily life.

Dealing with Reality

That way of life is a tremendous ideal, indeed! But how do we regain such an ideal when so much in our world militates against it? Our society is reeling from the devastating effects of pornography, sexual promiscuity, substance abuse, child and spouse abuse, and violent crime. And in spite of recent campaigns by special interest groups to regain the traditional values of American society, the family is threatened. What used to be considered an oasis of community, safety, and security is being eroded by society's ills. And, in many cases, the family is a breeding ground for the propagation of some of these threatening trends.

Moreover, the status of the American family is changing. The norm for family life is no longer dad, mom, kids, and the family pet, all living happily together in a nice, quiet neighborhood with other families of like composition. Many families lack quality contact within an extended family setting. Establishing family traditions and memories does not play as significant a role in family life as it once did. Divorce, single-parent families, latchkey kids, moms working outside the home, fewer children per household, and two-career marriages are all becoming increasingly common. Consequently, parenting and family nurture are becoming increasingly complex tasks.

Our style of living also threatens the stability of the family. The push of daily activity keeps families feeling fragmented and disoriented. Filtering significant communication through our busy schedules is problematic. The growing presence of electronic media in our homes is impinging on the ability of parents and children to share their lives together in any significant way.

Through it all, the family in our society has lost grasp of the ability to do things together; i.e., the kinds of things that create the context which permits the natural transmission of faith-in-life between parents and children. Many Christian families today need help in once again knowing how to express their faith in the natural flow of family relationships.

The natural place for parents to come for that help is the church. And, rightly so! The church, after all, represents the family in its larger spiritual and social dimensions. It is the one place where the family as a whole can be involved all at the same time. It is the one place where family values are still maintained and nurtured. Moreover, the strength of a church's families will inevitably dictate the health of the church. Why then wouldn't the local church want to enter into this important process of spiritual formation of the family?

How has the church done in facilitating this spiritual development and formation of the family? For the most part, the church as a whole has done a credible job of teaching adults how to live lives that are authentically Christian. Children are ministered to and brought to a point of experiencing Jesus Christ personally as Saviour and Lord. Programs abound for every age group in the church. "We are a family church," we say. "We have something for everyone."

But what about *families together?* What kind of experience do families share together in church? Each week families come into church and each family member goes his or her own way, not to see each other again until they pile into the car to go home. Families, especially parents, are left feeling out of touch with each other as a result of their Sunday morning experience. Consequently, the cry is often heard from the pew for more family togetherness and unity in the church.

In an attempt to create this sense of family togetherness and unity, the adult worship experience has become the program in focus. Often we attempt to make our worship experiences more palatable to our younger audience by offering children's stories and special bulletin inserts. Children come into the worship services loaded down with coloring books, story books, and other materials to keep them occupied so they do not disturb those around them.

Involving our children in the adult worship setting, though, has not really succeeded in assisting the family to become the minicommunity of faith that Deuteronomy 6 talks about. More often than not, we have only succeeded in complicating our worship structures. Neither have we made our worship experiences any more relevant to our children or youth.

We can do few things to alter the fact that our worship experiences are, by and large, adult experiences. In addition, from an educational perspective, the learning that takes place is both passive and highly individualized. The family unit as a whole is not actively involved together in the learning process. Discovery is largely due to personal motivation rather than through dialogue and interaction among the family members themselves. The values of creating family unity or providing a family experience are marginal. Generally, in the end, one or both parents spend as much time keeping the children busy as they do entering into the spirit of the service. And contrary to popular opinion, having children endure an adult worship service, "so they can learn to sit quietly in church," does not make a worship service a worthwhile family activity!

An Attractive Alternative

How, then, is the church helping families nurture those very basic relationships, spiritual and social, that assist the home in truly becoming a seedbed of faith? There must be a better way! I believe there is. But first, it needs to be said that we should not feel guilty about our age-group programming in the church. Gearing our ministries for the various needs of numerous groups is legitimate and biblical. But while we are doing well at ministering to individual family members, we generally do not do a very good job of ministering to the family unit as a whole.

So what is the solution? Well, how about *intergenerational learning groups?* While it is impractical, if not impossible, to structure a church so that families are kept together all the time, it is not out of the question to structure an occasional activity or a series of learning sessions in which whole families participate together around the Word of God.

Intergenerational learning is not a new idea. In fact, it goes back to Deuteronomy 6. Intergenerational learning is a time when families come together in an informal, guided format, and participate together in a learning activity or activities. Because it involves various ages in learning together, crossing lines of generations, it is called *intergenerational*. It can be one of the most rewarding experiences a church can provide for its families. For, while many adults are equipped to be parents, and equipped to be Christians, not as many are equipped to engage with their children in informal spiritual relationships (i.e., the kind described in Deuteronomy 6).

In an intergenerational learning setting, parents (and other adults) have the opportunity to lead their children in personal discovery and application of the truths of God's Word. Children have the opportunity to interact with parents (and other adults), allowing them to express their faith in a way that is consistent with who they are and what they are. A planned program of intergenerational learning experiences provides the kind of assistance and tools parents need to become involved with their children in a shared-faith relationship.

Benefits of Intergenerational Learning
There are tremendous benefits that can accrue for families and churches interested in pursuing an intergenerational learning program.

Transmission of faith. As previously stated, intergenerational learning provides the opportunity for parents to engage their children in informal conversation and activity around the Word of God. This is perhaps the most obvious benefit of intergenerational learning. The discovery of Bible truths is put back in the context of the family, rather than in an age-graded classroom. Through intergenerational learning the transmission of faith from parent to child is experienced in the natural flow of activity together. Parents can learn new and creative ways to transmit their faith to their children. It can also open up new horizons for a family interested in going beyond a traditional family devotional format in the home.

Sharpening relational skills. In an intergenerational learning ex-

15

perience family members have a chance to sharpen their relational skills. As they work together they will learn new things about each other. How each one thinks and feels, how each one processes information, what kind of skills each has — all come to light as they work together in an intergenerational learning setting. This knowledge can help family members express appreciation for each other, as well as assist them in learning new ways of relating to each other.

Recapturing the simplicity of faith. We live in a complex world. To make matters worse, we adults tend toward that which is complex. We can really make things much more complicated than they are! Unfortunately, our faith in Christ can take on some of that same character. It can become more complicated and cumbersome than it really is. Not so for children! One of the benefits of intergenerational learning is that it helps us recapture the simplicity of our faith in Jesus Christ.

Contrary to most adults, children approach faith in Christ in a way that is fresh, simple, and real. They have not lost the sense of wonder and mystery that we sophisticated adults sometimes neglect. Children can teach us much about the simplicity of our faith — and they do when we join together with them in an intergenerational learning setting.

Family bonding. In a world that is increasingly fragmented, intergenerational learning offers the opportunity for families to grow closer together. In an intergenerational learning experience a family has the opportunity to practice the basic skills necessary for strong family relationships. Listening, cooperation, and conversation are all part of everyday life in the family. These are also necessary for a family to practice in order to maintain a bond of unity in the home. Intergenerational learning experiences provide a forum for families to practice these essential skills for keeping their family ties strong.

Modeling. Children need the benefit of observing adults practice their faith. Families need to see other families work out their faith together in the flow of informal activity. Intergenerational learning provides for both of these needs. Younger participants can see and hear older participants express and practice their commitments to Jesus Christ. A model is provided from which children can establish their own faith commitments. The same is true between families. In an intergenerational learning setting families can observe and learn from each other regarding family relationships and faith relationships.

Congregational growth and stability. When families join together in an intergenerational learning experience, a new sense of life and joy is likely to result. Families will grow together in their Christian faith. They will become excited about what they are learning and experiencing. Unity between individuals and families will be strengthened. Little of this can happen without having an impact on the congregation as a whole. Joy, excitement, and growth resulting from experiential learning are all contagious within a congregation. And as families are being strengthened and built up, it will inevitably be felt within the life of a congregation.

Postscript

The more complex our society becomes the more the church will need to evaluate its ministry to families. Indeed, it will become imperative. But we will need to go beyond the traditional strategies of offering Sunday School courses, seminars, counseling programs, and parent support groups. While these traditional strategies are good, the real need of assisting families in the process of spiritual formation is often addressed in an academic environment, leaving out a most important key element: opportunities for intergenerational involvements and family interaction.

If we are to be effective in assisting Christian families in the process of spiritual formation, we will need to provide program strategies that are creative and that go beyond the generally accepted church-time programs. That is to say, our strategies will need to provide for a Deuteronomy 6 style of interaction within families and across generational lines. A program of family/intergenerational learning is one such strategy.

17

TWO

How and Where
to Begin

I enjoy landscaping. In fact, it is kind of a hobby. When Judy and I first moved to Pennsylvania several years ago, we found ourselves in a brand-new house in a brand-new housing development. It was all very exciting! But the most exciting thing for me was the prospect of planning my own landscape design. A basic design was already established by the developer, consisting of a freshly seeded lawn, a few shrubs, and a couple of trees. But most of the designing and work I did myself. I did research to find out how to properly establish a new lawn, what types of bushes and trees would work well in my yard with its particular soil. I visited nurseries to survey my options. After all, not just any bush would do!

I spent hours plotting and planning. I planted trees, hauled dirt, mulched shrubbery beds, and fed and weeded the lawn. And after about two and one-half years the process was finally completed when I planted the last two trees in the backyard. It was landscape heaven! At least, that was how it appeared to me.

So what does all this have to do with intergenerational learning in the church? It is really very simple. Planning to do inter-generational learning in your church is much like plotting a landscape design. For all of my grand visions of creating a land-scape heaven, getting started was the most difficult part. Know-ing where to go, whom to talk to, how to proceed, what combi-nations would work best, were all very important considerations if I wanted my vision to be fully realized in the final product.

So it is with developing a ministry of intergenerational learn-ing in your church. Getting started is often the most difficult part. Much of what you do before you ever conduct a session will have great bearing on how the finished product will look. Knowing where to go, how to proceed, what combination of ingredients will work best, are important considerations for de-veloping an effective intergenerational learning program. The following steps will help you as you begin the process of plotting the landscape of your intergenerational learning program.

Step One: Do Your Homework

Having a basic understanding of the how's and why's of inter-generational learning will greatly enhance your ability to lead in intergenerational learning. Hence, you should spend some time reading and doing research. Ask yourself some questions as you begin. Questions like: What is intergenerational learning? What does it involve? What are the benefits and the risks? Take time to get comfortable with the idea. While you may be excited about the possibilities of intergenerational learning, there is no need to rush into doing it right away.

I once had a college professor who told me, "If it's worth doing, then it's worth doing well!" That was good advice for me as a college student, and it has become equally as valuable for me as a pastor. If you believe intergenerational learning is im-portant for your church, then it is important enough to spend the time doing your homework to understand what it involves. Let the vision of the ministry grow in your own mind until you are thoroughly excited about it. You will be better able to com-municate desires and plans if you first understand it.

Research and study can take many forms. The first and most obvious form of research is reading. There are many printed resources available that can help you establish a basic under-standing of intergenerational learning. Many of the resources listed at the back of this book can provide you with a comprehensive theology of intergenerational learning in the church.

A second form of research involves talking with others who have done intergenerational learning. I found early on in ministry, learning from others' mistakes was much more comfortable than learning from my own! Find someone who has led intergenerational learning experiences and pick his or her brain. Find out all you can from that person. Some good questions to ask would be:

- How did you get started?
- What has worked best for you?
- What has not worked so well?
- What possibilities for intergenerational learning do you see in the church?
- What kind of settings have you used?
- What material have you used? Where can I find it?
- What benefits or risks do you see in intergenerational learning?
- What have you learned about intergenerational learning?
- How should I go about getting started?

These questions should give you some good handles on knowing how to proceed in planning your own intergenerational learning experiences.

A third form of research, far more valuable than anything else you could do, is participation. That is, find someone who is planning to do an intergenerational learning time and ask them if you can participate in the session. If they are doing more than one session, you could possibly become involved in the planning process with them. Or better yet, perhaps they would be willing to let you assume some leadership responsibilities during a session. My first real exposure with intergenerational learning was just this kind of experience. I think I learned far more through this kind of exposure than through any other means since.

If no one you know is doing intergenerational learning, perhaps you can ask someone to come and do a model session for you in your own church. Or perhaps they would be willing to conduct a session in their church so you can observe. This would give you a feel for how an intergenerational session works.

One thing about research by participation, be sure to allow

time to debrief with the leader after it is over. In my first experience we would meet as a planning team after each session, evaluate how it went, and then plan the next one. A period of debriefing will let you process what you have just experienced. There is something that happens in the learning process when we allow time for immediate reflection. Reflection and evaluation while an experience is still fresh can sometimes yield far greater insight than waiting until later.

Step Two: Approach Church Leadership

When the vision for intergenerational learning has thoroughly gripped you, then talk to your church's leadership about your desires. Share what you have experienced and learned. Discuss with them the benefits of intergenerational learning experiences for your church. Solicit their support and involvement. If at all possible let your plans be sponsored by an established leadership group, such as your Christian Education board, or some other official group that would have appropriate oversight of such projects.

Generally, there is automatic strength of support for a new program when it comes from an established leadership group rather than from an individual. The support and involvement of church leadership will enhance the desirability of intergenerational learning in your church, as well as give your program credibility.

Step Three: Plan Your Program

Once you have received the support from the appropriate church leadership, your next step will be to plan your program. In planning your program you will need to answer the following questions:

- Are you planning for a multi-session series, a single-session experience, or both?
- How many and what kind of experiences will you have in a given year?
- When will you be holding these sessions?
- If you are running a series, how long will it run?
- Look at the church calendar. Will there be any conflicts with other significant church activities?
- What day will you conduct your learning sessions?

- What time will you begin and end?
- Who will be invited to participate — the entire congregation or a specific target group?
- What program can you drop or suspend to free up time for the whole family to participate?

Once you have answered these questions you are well on your way to running an effective program of intergenerational learning.

A question I hear often is, "How do we plug this into our church program? Our church calendar is already so full just with regular service activities. What would be the best time and setting for this kind of program?" My answer is usually quite simple. There is really no best time for doing intergenerational learning. Any time you would like to do it, and think it will work, is the best time.

I have conducted sessions in just about every major time slot in the church program calendar. I have conducted sessions after the Sunday evening service and as a study option on Wednesday evening. My first experience was during the Sunday School hour. When I pastored a church in the Midwest, we ran a summer series during the Sunday evening service time. All other Sunday evening programs were set aside during that time so families were free to participate. Being a small church was an obvious advantage in that situation.

Intergenerational programming offers a break from the traditional church educational system, allowing families a chance to focus on their own spiritual nurture in a concentrated way. It can be short-term or long-term. It can be a single session on a special holiday. Or, it can be a series ranging from 3 to 13 sessions, or longer. It is supplemental to the overall Christian Education and family nurture ministries of the church. It can, therefore, be integrated into the church's program schedule with minimal disruption.

Hence, the options for when to do intergenerational learning are limited only by the needs of your immediate situation. Consider some of these options:

- As a quarter-long Sunday School elective
- As a week-long family camp
- As a weekend family retreat
- As a Sunday or Wednesday evening service option

- As an occasional, single-evening church family night
- In a small group consisting of several families
- Before or after Sunday or Wednesday evening service
- As a special family event during Thanksgiving, Christmas, or Lenten Season
- As a special activity or series during Vacation Bible School

When you run your program will be an important factor, especially if this is a first for your church. You will want to plan to allow as many as possible the chance to attend. If you are planning an experience for a special target group, you will want to be sure that as many from that group as possible have the opportunity to attend. In other words, do not run a session or series at a time you will be excluding a significant number of those you desire to see attend. If you only want a smaller group to participate, then you are free to choose a time that you feel will be suitable. Whichever the case, planning wisely will contribute to the success of your program.

Step Four: Select Your Materials

Choosing your materials will perhaps be the most difficult chore. Basically you have several choices. You can either buy prepared materials, you can write your own, you can use those written by someone you know who has done intergenerational learning, or any combination of these. Currently, there are a number of good materials available. Those found in this book, or noted in the reference listing, are obviously strong possibilities.

If you feel more comfortable writing your own, then go for it! It can be fun and rewarding. I started out writing my own because at the time I was not satisfied with what was on the market. Fortunately, this has changed. I have also found that there are others doing intergenerational learning who have likewise developed their own materials. These can be excellent resources if you can tap into them.

As you choose your materials, examine them carefully to determine if they suit the needs of your church and the goals of your learning program.

Step Five: Assemble a Leadership Team

There is an old saying: "Many hands make light work." We could paraphrase that to say, "Many hands make more enthusiasm"! The broader the congregational involvement in planning and implementing your program the more enthusiastic the congregation will be in receiving it. Generally speaking, vision and morale in ministry are directly proportionate to the levels of congregational involvement and participation. This is likewise true of intergenerational learning.

Assemble a team of interested adults who can help plan and lead the learning sessions with you. Intergenerational learning takes a lot of time and work to prepare for and implement. Moreover, involving others is a good way to multiply yourself in ministry as others will be equipped to lead in a growing and developing intergenerational learning program.

As you assemble your team it will be far more effective to approach people individually rather than just giving a general announcement. Think in terms of what people do well so you can build on each others' strengths. As your team comes together you will need to orient and brief them as to your plans. Share the vision of intergenerational learning with them. Let them catch your enthusiasm. Explain what will happen in a typical session. Talk through a session to let them get a feel for how it will work. Then begin the process of planning and giving assignments.

My first experience in intergenerational learning was with a team. Each week we would meet and assignments would be made for the next session. Someone was in charge of music, another was responsible for the Bible story presentation, someone else was to lead a discussion activity, and others were responsible for the learning centers. In addition, as we would talk through the next session we would think of different ways to present the Bible story, or generate a different idea for a family project or readiness activity.

As a leader you will find that team planning multiplies creativity. It also will relieve you of a lot of work! But more importantly, it will broaden the base of congregational involvement in an important ministry, and enthusiasm will filter down through team members to the rest of the congregation.

Step Six: Promote Your Program
Great planning accomplishes little if you do not inform the congregation of your plans. Use every available means in the

congregation to inform them of the planned program. Begin well in advance.

It never ceases to amaze me how much we take promotion for granted in the church. We somehow mistakenly think that just because it is a church activity we should not have to promote it very much. Last-minute announcements are deemed adequate. But the fact of reality is, if you want people to be involved you need to give them enough time to plan to be involved, especially if you are conducting your session(s) at a time other than a regular church-time program hour.

The way you promote your program is limited only by your imagination. In fact, a good rule of thumb is, "Leave no stone unturned"! Promotion can really become both creative and fun. Think of ways to go beyond the typical bulletin announcement. For instance, recruit four people to do a skit during announcement time in the morning worship service. Designate two of them as parents and the other two as children. Then present a caricature of Mom and Dad trying to keep their children occupied in a morning service. Or, have someone wear a sandwich sign and roam through the foyer on a Sunday morning handing out "free tickets." Testimonials and interviews from those having participated in an intergenerational experience can also be very effective.

If this is a totally new concept for your congregation, perhaps you could conduct a brief sample session after an evening service, or during the Wednesday evening time. It would not have to be a whole session. Select parts from a session that will give people enough of an idea to make an informed decision about being involved.

If you are running a multisession series, use what you do in the session time as a way to promote both the series and the concept of intergenerational learning. In one church, after the first session, the Senior Pastor and I planned to wear our name tags during the announcement time in the worship service. That may not sound like much, but the name tags were large pieces of construction paper that were hung around our necks with a piece of yarn! In another church we posted the banners families made illustrating the message of the parable of the lost sheep. After two weeks the banners were returned to the families.

Let your leadership team help you plan your promotion.

When people put their heads together and begin bouncing ideas around, all kinds of creative things can happen.

One more important thing you need to know about promotion. Be sure to communicate expectations of what you will be doing together. I was recently talking with a friend who had just conducted a week-long family camp. He made the interesting observation that, "People have to be mentally prepared before starting." He said that for those who had no exposure to inter-generational learning it was "strange city"! Fear and anxiety were noticeable, especially where families did not seem to know how to talk to each other, and particularly when it involved parents and older children. His conclusion was, "Families aren't prepared to be nurtured as families." He also concluded that the next time he will use his own family to demonstrate an activity, to show simple ways to talk and work together.

This was instructive for me. It underscored the importance of letting people know what they will be doing if they choose to participate. They will be expected to work together as families. They will need to be able to talk with each other as they work on the various projects. Parents will need to be able to assume leadership of their families. Children will be expected to work with their families rather than running helter-skelter through the room. As you promote your program, you will need to orient people so that they can, as my friend said, be mentally prepared and comfortable with the concept before they start.

Step Seven: Logistical Considerations
There is a great deal more to planning an intergenerational learning program than just choosing materials, setting dates, and doing promotion. There are several logistical considerations you need to take into account if you want your program to be effective.

Time. How long will your sessions last? A good length is from 60 to 75 minutes. This allows ample time to complete any activities you desire to do in each session. But neither is it too long. When young children are involved time is an important factor. Moreover, the nature of your sessions dictates not going too long. Too much activity can get both tiring and boring.

Facility. Do you have a room big enough to accommodate the number of people you expect? Is there adequate lighting and ventilation? Does your room encourage or prohibit interaction? Does it promote a warm learning environment? In order to facilitate an effective intergenerational learning session your meeting area will need to have space for the large group to be together, in addition to areas for families to work on projects. While there are many ways to "make space" by the way you set up your equipment and facilities, a room too small is still too small!

There is no one ideal way to set up a room. I personally prefer a table at the entrance for the readiness activity, work tables around the outside of the room, with a table for supplies at one end. The center area is set up with a large semicircle of chairs, leaving room for children and others to sit on the floor if it is carpeted. If not, children can then sit on chairs next to their parents. This arrangement leaves plenty of space in the front of the room for you and your leadership team to work.

This is what I prefer. I have not always had what I prefer. One family camp I conducted had *no* inside facility. Hence, the group sat outside on lawn chairs and blankets on the ground. We used a picnic table for our supply center. Families sat on blankets to complete their projects. Of course being outside also meant I could not use electrical audiovisual equipment. So I improvised with a homemade flip chart.

Doing intergenerational learning in that setting was a challenge, but it was also fun. While you may not always have the ideal facility making the best use of what you do have will be a good test of your ingenuity. To say it another way, flexibility and creativity are the keys to working with your physical plant.

Equipment. Do you have enough chairs? How about tables? Is there a chalkboard and bulletin board in the meeting area that can be easily used during your large group times? Can you set up a projection screen, overhead projector, and filmstrip projector? Do you have enough extension cords and electrical outlets?

Ideally, your room should have space to set up all your audiovisual equipment at one time, a bulletin board and/or chalkboard easy to use and see during the large group times, and enough tables and chairs to accommodate the largest group possible. A large portable chalkboard or bulletin board is the best. This will give you greater versatility in setting up your learning area.

Supplies. Are you and your church able to provide all of the craft items necessary for the learning projects? Again, do not take anything for granted. It is a good idea to take inventory before you begin. It is also a good idea to try to have most of what you need before you begin.

In most cases this will not be a problem. Most churches have a resource room or storage cabinets used to keep various classroom supplies for Sunday School and other programs. Work with those in charge of this area to collect your supplies. If there is a budget line for such items be sure to work out the necessary details of purchasing supplies as needed.

If you do not have either a resource area or budget for supplies, you have three options. You can purchase your own, which of course can be quite costly. You can request that a special budget line be established to procure necessary items. Or, you can ask people in the congregation to donate.

When we conducted our summer series in the small church in the Midwest, there were several items in particular we were going to need; specifically, magazines, wire clothes hangers, and tin cans. I put a request to the congregation for people to donate. Boxes were placed in the church foyer as collection points. The response was overwhelming. One woman found several bunches of hangers at a yard sale for only a quarter a bunch. Another woman brought tin cans from the kitchen of the daycare center where she worked. And everyone, it seemed, wanted to rid their house of the growing stack of old magazines. We had more hangers, cans, and magazines than we needed!

From that experience I learned that when you ask people to donate you help create enthusiasm and interest. People have the opportunity to make a personal investment even before they participate in a session. Their involvement level is heightened, and they develop ownership of the program. If you or your church do not have all the finances to purchase all the necessary supplies, do not overlook this option. There are many hidden benefits to be gained.

In Conclusion

Knowing how to get a new project started is very important. But knowing what to do after you get started is equally as important. As I learned in landscaping, it is one thing to know how to dig a hole. Knowing how to plant a tree in the same hole is quite another matter! Moving a new project from the point of beginning to the point of completion is seldom a matter of one giant step. It is a result of many small steps.

The steps given in this chapter are just that, small steps that will help you bring your desires to do intergenerational learning from the point of beginning to the point of completion. Hopefully, these steps represent a logical, intentional sequence of actions that will help you realize your vision for intergenerational learning in your church.

THREE

Basic Components in Intergenerational Learning

When I was in the midst of plotting the landscape design for my new house I learned a very important lesson about balance and symmetry. Balance and symmetry are important aspects to gaining a visually appealing landscape design. They are achieved by how you organize some very basic components; more specifically, the color, height, size, type, and placement of the raw materials. How these components are organized will determine the balance and symmetry of your design, and enhance its appeal.

Balance and symmetry are important principles for planning a program of intergenerational learning also. Several basic components are necessary which, if included and properly utilized, will add to the effectiveness and appeal of your program. There are five such components important to include as you plan your learning sessions.

Basic Component One: Activity
Involving generations together in any learning time requires a format that will involve all those of various ages together in a

meaningful way. I have noticed that some materials for intergenerational learning tend to structure sessions around dialogue. Other materials are geared toward didactic instruction. Making dialogue or didactic instruction your primary approach in your learning sessions, however, will not be taking into account two important issues of intergenerational learning.

First, there is the matter of the needs of learners and the way people learn best. Planning sessions around dialogue and didactic instruction may work well in a group of adults. But in intergenerational learning you are planning for more than just adults. Teens and children both need learning experiences that provide activity. Even adults learn best by doing. All of us learn best when we are directly and actively involved in the learning process. Active learning, characterized by an activity approach, will allow you to reach across generational lines and provide the best learning experiences for all ages.

The second issue relates to your purpose in intergenerational learning. Your concern should be to have generations involved together in the learning process. Therefore, you need to establish a common frame of reference for interaction. Activities that are dialogical or didactic may make your adults feel more comfortable, but it will not necessarily stimulate conversation between family members. Planning sessions that are activity oriented helps provide learning experiences that allow for interaction between members of families and across generational lines.

Activity in itself stimulates conversation, if for no other reason than family members will have to talk to and cooperate with each other in order to complete the learning activity. But, at a deeper level, sharing together in an activity can lead to significant informal conversation about the meaning of the activity and message of the Bible focus. It creates an environment in which children and adults alike ask questions and freely respond to each other. Learning and sharing are mutually experienced rather than just a one-way "telling" from adult to child.

It has been a great privilege for me to observe families working together on a learning activity, and listening as parents respond to questions their children ask, "Why does this go here, Mom? What is this for, Dad?" What a thrilling experience to be able to see parents and children talking with each other concerning issues of faith-in-life coming from the natural flow of doing an activity together.

As a father of two young children, I am especially excited when I see other fathers conversing freely and informally with their own children regarding these issues of faith-in-life. As I have had the opportunity to observe their interaction, I have often thought it reminiscent of Paul's words to the Thessalonians, "For you know that we dealt with each of you as a father deals with his own children, encouraging, comforting, and urging you to live lives worthy of God, who calls you into His kingdom and glory" (1 Thes. 2:11-12). That is the heart of Deuteronomy 6:5-9, and it is likewise the heart of intergenerational learning.

Basic Component Two: Simplicity

Intergenerational learning does not have to be complex. Trying to plan sessions that are unique, "really neat," or elaborate may leave your participants wondering about the value of their time together. While your activities need to be interesting and substantial in content, they need not be difficult or complex. Remember, you are planning for a diversity of ages, experiences, and abilities. You will need to be careful not to inadvertently exclude individuals by planning activities they are unable to complete.

When I first became involved in intergenerational learning in seminary, our instructor suggested that we should gear our activities so that the youngest person involved could do them. After seminary I was discussing this concern with an individual who was involved in a small group for families. When I suggested he gear his activities to the youngest child in attendance, his response was, "But what do the rest of us do? We have been doing that, but things are starting to get a little boring for the others, especially the older children."

Since then, and from my own experiences, I have modified my thinking. I believe a good rule of thumb is: *Plan activities that even the youngest family members are able to participate in with help from older family members.* In other words, within any well-planned activity there should be distinguishable levels of involvement. While a child may not be able to sketch a project pattern, he can cut out paper shapes, or color, or help glue things down. A senior adult may not have the manual dexterity to cut out small intricate shapes, but he can give significant conceptual guidance for a learning project. Even though a young child cannot sing along during group songs, he can enjoy the fun of clapping and bouncing on his parent's knee. While an adult may be too inhibited to participate in a skit or a puppet presentation, teenagers can be natural actors, while everyone enjoys watching and laughing at what they see. In other words, your session activity needs to allow all participants the opportunity to be involved at various levels of experience.

Basic Component Three: Informality

Active, simple learning experiences help create an atmosphere that tends to be loose and relaxed. That's good! The value of intergenerational learning is greatly enhanced when you keep an informal environment. Letting children sit on the floor is not out of the question. Laughing is good. Dressing in jeans and tennis shoes is not bad. As leader, you are the key to informality. How you dress, act, and carry yourself will greatly determine how at ease and comfortable the rest of the group will feel.

The physical arrangements of the room will also help in creating a relaxed environment. Having chairs in rows can create a stiff and sterile environment. Standing behind a podium may make you feel out of reach and aloof from the group experience.

Informal, however, does not mean *unstructured.* And it especially does not mean *unplanned.* Your sessions will need to have some structure in order for them to flow smoothly. Careful planning and a definite format are both essential for creating healthy and rewarding learning experiences. But it is not necessary to adopt stained-glass manners! Enjoy yourself and let others enjoy themselves. They will thank you for it.

Basic Component Four: Celebration

Let your people celebrate! There is nothing wrong with having fun in fellowship with other believers, especially when you are gathered around the Word of God. Let your times together be characterized by celebrating the life of God. Again, you as leader are the key here. Don't be stale, stiff, and boring. Your participants will enjoy their time together only as much as you do. They will seldom celebrate more than you.

We have much to celebrate in the life God has given us through Jesus Christ. Your time together should reflect this reality. Read Revelation 19:1-9 in your Bible. Let the vision of the heavenly celebration be your model. In that celebration we will be gathering as one family for the glory of Jesus Christ. So just consider your time together as getting a little head start on the celebration!

Basic Component Five: Involvement
While this may sound obvious, once again, take nothing for granted. There are three levels of involvement to which you will want to be attentive.

Nuclear families. First, your families are there to be involved, but will they be involved together? Plan your time so that nuclear families are involved together in the learning activities. Encourage the older family members to help the younger ones. Encourage parents to work with their children, not just manage the activities for their children by telling them what to do or by doing it for them.

Extended families and family clusters. The second level of involvement goes beyond the nuclear family. What about singles who may attend? Or elderly couples? Or couples without children? Will they feel comfortable attending and doing learning projects on their own? Should they be encouraged to attend? My answer to these questions is, "Yes!" Let them be included, seniors and singles alike.

Intergenerational learning is not just for nuclear families. By definition, intergenerational learning is for everyone of all ages. Some singles, elderly couples, and even most couples without children, will feel quite comfortable working on their own learning projects alone. In fact, in one family camp I conducted one elderly couple insisted on doing their own project, even though their son and his family were participating also. They wanted the fun of doing it with just each other. In another church, there was a single who worked on his own projects throughout much of the series. On other projects he would work with another family who "adopted" him as an extra "uncle."

Do not underestimate your people. You may be surprised at how many will want to participate and work on their own learning projects, even though they are not married or have no children. I would, however, suggest that you encourage those singles and couples, elderly or without children, who are comfortable working on projects alone to work alongside another family. Let them benefit from the interaction of multiple generations while completing their own learning activity.

There may be those singles, elderly couples, or couples without children who do not feel comfortable working alone. Some of them may be too shy to say so. You will need to find creative ways to integrate these couples or individuals into the learning process so they are not unintentionally left out. Several options are available. One option is the extended family approach. In some cases you may have families participating that run the gamut of ages from young child to grandparent. It is natural then for grandma and grandpa to be involved with their children and grandchildren.

Another option is for a smaller family to "adopt" an extra set of grandparents for the duration of the session or series. Or, perhaps they could "adopt" an extra son or daughter, or aunt or uncle.

A third option is to involve several senior couples together as a family unit. In one church where we were doing an intergenerational learning series, several senior couples took this approach. It worked out very well. They enjoyed the opportunity to work together, as well as the stimulating interaction that resulted from working on the learning activities.

A last option is to encourage singles, elderly couples, and couples without children to form their own extended families and stay together throughout your time together.

Session participation. A third level of involvement has to do with the session itself. Is it necessary for the leader to do everything? Gather a team of workers together. Let one person handle the music, and another the learning activities. Involve group members in the story presentation as much as possible. Have someone else do the discussion exercise. The greater the level of involvement the greater the value of learning and sharing. Involvement creates a greater continuity of group experience and relationship. It also creates a high level of group morale and excitement. Without the continuity and morale which come from involvement, your time together could end up being dull and unexciting.

In Summary

It is difficult to be too young or too old to be involved in intergenerational learning times. But involvement must not be taken for granted. As you plan and implement your sessions, take steps to insure that those who are participating are actively involved, not just passive observers. Keep your atmosphere relaxed and informal. Plan meaningful activities. And above all, celebrate!

FOUR

Organizing Your Learning Session

So, you are ready to begin! You gather a group of people together for your first intergenerational learning session. What now? If you are using a prepared curriculum your session format should be outlined for you already. Sometimes, however, the outlines of some materials leave a bit to be desired. So permit me to suggest a basic five-part session format that reflects the concerns expressed in the previous chapter. This format is not original with myself. It is like the outline we used in my seminary experience. Since then, I have used it extensively with various adaptations and modifications along the way. I believe it will offer you the greatest versatility in whatever setting you may find yourself and with any material you choose to use.

Part One: Readiness Activity

This is the period of time just before the session actually begins. People are arriving in the room, orienting themselves to the surroundings, and generally trying to settle themselves for the session. The readiness activity is an important time for getting your participants involved with each other. Its purposes are to get the families mingling together as soon as they arrive, prepare them for the theme of the session, and to allow them the opportunity to get acquainted with other families. There are several different kinds of readiness activities you can use.

Name Tags. Perhaps the easiest and most beneficial readiness activity is the name tag. As families arrive each member can make a name tag from a half sheet of construction paper, punch holes in the top corners, tie a piece of yarn through the holes, and hang it around his or her neck. The name tag should display the person's first name.

Other information can be put on the name tag as well. Participants could draw a picture telling others something about themselves; e.g., a hobby, something they enjoy doing, something they did on a recent vacation, etc. Or, they could put something on their name tag that is related to your session theme. For instance, if your session is about the Parable of the Sower, have each person write the reference to a Scripture verse or verses they can quote. Then have them move around the room and share their verse(s) with each other.

Bulletin Boards. Another simple readiness activity is a bulletin board decoration. As families arrive direct them to complete a piece to be posted on the bulletin board. Preferably, the bulletin board theme would match the theme of your session.

For example, if your theme is on helping, taken from the Parable of the Good Samaritan, put a heading on the bulletin board called "Ours Are Helping Hands." In the middle of the board post a giant silhouette of a hand. As people arrive direct them to trace one of their hands on construction paper, cut it out, and staple it on or around the large silhouette.

Bulletin boards do not have to be complex. They can be quite simple in design and concept. The bulletin boards made by the group can then be left up for several sessions.

Door Decorations. Door decorations would work much the same way as a bulletin board design. As families arrive they would have an opportunity to contribute to a predetermined decoration theme. Door decorations could also carry seasonal or holiday themes.

Murals. Murals are a bit more involved than the previous three ideas, but they can be just as much fun. To make one you need to supply a basic background for a particular scene you want to create in your mural. As families arrive they would add the necessary details to complete the scene. Your mural could be theme related, depicting a simple scene from the Bible story you are using in that session. Or, it could take on a holiday or seasonal flavor. Sometimes these two angles can be blended together.

Mosaic and stained-glass window designs can be used very effectively in group mural building. An even simpler way to build a mural would be to have families color in parts of the scene with crayons. Obviously, using either of these approaches for a mural would require you to trace a full outline of the scene you want completed.

Token Gifts. A token gift is something simple each person or family can make and give to someone else in the group. A "warm fuzzy" made from chenille wire, a tissue paper carnation, a smiley face made from yellow construction paper, a button-hole flower made from pipe cleaners and construction paper, a simple message written on a marker tag and hung on a person's shirt button with a piece of string—all are simple and good tokens easily made and fun to give. These kinds of things are especially good if you are doing a session on reaching out, loving others, or encouraging others. They can also be used effectively during a special holiday season or for other special days, such as Mother's or Father's Day.

These ideas for readiness activities are by no means exhaustive. Readiness activities can take many forms. Feel free to experiment. The point is, your readiness activity will help create a warm, comfortable, and open atmosphere for your learning session. You should set up your readiness activity on a table near the entrance of the room with all the necessary materials, and a large, simple, easy-to-read instruction card. This will engage families in the activity as soon as they come into the room.

Part Two: Group Time
When it is time to begin your session, your Group Time will be the first thing you do. Your families will gather together to do several very important things.

Introduction. Group Time begins with the session leader welcoming the group, introducing himself or herself, briefly outlining the unit theme, and introducing the theme for that session. Be creative in introducing your theme. Use object lessons or short group exercises to grab people's attention. If you are doing a multisession series you could also take a few minutes to briefly review the previous session theme to help maintain a sense of continuity in the series, especially for those who might have missed a session.

Music. The group is then led in several songs related to your session theme. Music plays a vital role in creating a greater continuity of group experience. While it is not necessary for you to be a musician to lead group singing, you do need to choose your songs wisely. I am not musically illiterate, but neither do I consider myself a musician. When I lead singing it is mostly done without accompaniment. Hence, easy-to-follow choruses, Scripture songs, and activity songs are more my style.

There are many options available for using music in your learning sessions. In one situation, I recruited a music leader who used a sing-along tape with a double track. She could tune out the singing, leaving an easy-to-follow accompaniment. Another helper played the piano quite well and was comfortable leading singing from the piano bench. In one family camp situation we had an appointed music leader who was very proficient leading singing with a guitar.

Whichever approach you use, you should always try to make sure your audience has access to the words of the songs. People are uncomfortable when they have to grope for words while singing. I prefer to project the words from an overhead projector onto a screen, even when singing simple choruses. Writing the words on a chalkboard or poster board can work well, so long as the letters are legible and large enough to be seen by the whole group. Handouts or chorus books can also be helpful. Using a printed source has another advantage. Parents can interact with their children while singing by pointing to individual words on the page.

The way you use music in your intergenerational sessions is simply a matter of discovering your own style and the options available within your own congregation. The key to using music is to use active, fun, easy-to-sing songs that both children and adults can enjoy. Scripture choruses are excellent. Certain hymns are not bad if used with discretion. Too many simplistic children's songs can wear on the adults. Try to strike a balance. You want your music to help people feel comfortable, open them up for learning, and help them praise and worship God.

Bible Story Presentation. A third important part of the Group Time is the presentation of the Bible story. Various forms of presentation can be used, especially in a multisession series. Consider some of the following methods.

● *Filmstrips.* Filmstrips are an enduring favorite for Bible story presentation in Christian Education. Many excellent sources for filmstrips are available. The resource listing in the back of this book can give you some sources to help you locate filmstrips. You can also make your own filmstrips. There are companies that supply blank filmstrip material, or you can make your own by rinsing an old filmstrip off with bleach and hanging it in the sun to dry.

● *Overhead Projector.* One of the most overlooked forms for story presentation is the overhead projector. With a bit of creativity you can make simple and appealing story pictures to use in presenting your Bible story. If you do not consider yourself an artist, then trace your pictures from simple Bible story books or Bible coloring books. You can also purchase story presentations for the overhead projector. See the resource listing in the back of this book for possible sources. If you choose to make your own try to keep the number of transparencies to ten or less. Any more than ten can be cumbersome to handle.

● *Simultaneous Mime.* A good method involving some of your participants is simultaneous mime. This is a method in which one person reads or tells the story, and others act out the story without speaking. Reading and acting are done simultaneously. This is a great way to involve members of your group in the presentation of the Bible story. No practice is required. They only have to listen to what is said and do it!

You may, however, need to rewrite the story in your own words so that the action the actors are to take is obvious. For example, in the Parable of the Prodigal Son, you could say, "The older brother, looking very angry, shook his finger in his father's face and said. . . ." Modern Bible paraphrases, children's Bible story books, and children's Sunday School or church-time curriculums are excellent sources for story scripts to work with simultaneous mime.

• *Puppet Drama.* Puppets are also a great way to present your Bible story. While a minimum of props and equipment are necessary, it will be well worth the effort. The basic props are the puppets and some kind of stage. If you don't have any puppets, try making your own out of paper lunch sacks. Stick or sock puppets can also be used effectively. For a stage, a curtain held by two people, a sheet of newsprint spread between two chairs or taped to a long table front, or a large table turned on its side are all easy ways to make a puppet stage front.

In presenting your story you can write your own script, use a paraphrase version of the Bible, or even read it from a Bible story book.

Options for telling the story go beyond the puppets doing the talking. Simultaneous mime works well with puppets. Using a cassette tape of the story is also an attractive option. Your puppeteers can even record the script on a cassette tape themselves.

• *Group Drama.* Group acting is another good method of involving the entire group in the storytelling process. It involves one person telling the story, with the key characters acting in simultaneous mime, while the group becomes the environment for the story. For instance, in the story of the calming of the storm you can have one person as Jesus, three or four as disciples, and the rest of the group circle around them as the storm itself; i.e., some making the sound of wind, others the waves, another group thundering, etc. As you tell the story, each group or actor follows the instructions given in the story line.

• *Skit.* An additional form of drama is the skit. Skits are simple and easy to do. Little or no practice is required. Actors can read the script. Memorization is not necessary. You will need to have a copy of the script for each person involved in the skit.

The actions performers are to take, along with the spoken lines, will need to be in the script. Many stories in the Bible are easy to script and make for great storytelling through skits.

• *Slides.* A form of story presentation often neglected is the slide presentation. A simple slide presentation can be made by using write-on slides. Or, a group of people can pose in costume for still shots with a camera. Your presentation would follow the same format as that of a filmstrip presentation. If you plan far enough in advance you could record your script on a cassette tape with music background, using people from your group as the various characters' voices. The same people could also read the script "live" during the presentation.

Whichever form of story presentation you use, let me say a word about story scripts. It is important that you do more than simply read the story from your Bible. Make the Bible come alive for your people! Stories that are real and alive will have a greater impact and enhance the learning process.

Writing the story to tell in your own words is always beneficial. If, however, you do not feel yourself to be a writer, there are many resources available that go beyond simply reading the story out of the Bible. Sunday School and children's church materials are great resources for action stories and rhymes which are very adaptable for simultaneous mime, skits, or puppets. Bible story books are also good resources for story scripts, with some modifications. A Bible paraphrase can also be used effectively for story presentation.

It takes time to develop good creative story presentations. But watching the Bible come alive for your people will be more than enough reward for your efforts!

Part Three: Family Discovery Time

After the story has been presented, the group then breaks into family units for Family Discovery Time. Two important things are accomplished during this time.

Creative Projects. Each family completes a creative project which reinforces the theme of the Bible story. Tables will need to be set up for family work spaces. You will also need a central materials table. You will need to have all the materials on hand necessary for completing the projects. The values of discovery time are family interaction, creative expression, and active learning.

When I first began doing intergenerational learning I tried various approaches for the family project time. First I tried work centers, where families worked in groups on a specific project, with each group having a different assignment. I noted, however, where more than one family worked together on a project, the more assertive individuals would dominate the work while the more passive ones would simply watch. In other cases the parents would sometimes sit back and simply tell their children what to do while they would engage in small talk.

I also tried using the learning center approach, instructing each family unit to complete a project from several possible choices, or to complete more than one simple project dealing with different aspects of the session theme. I began observing that some families were unsure and uncomfortable at having to choose their activity, while some would choose very quickly. Where they were instructed to choose more than one project to complete, some families would move very fast, while others wandered around a bit from table to table seemingly lost and somewhat frustrated from a lack of structure.

As a result, I have settled on a more structured approach that I believe has more benefit all the way around. I use one creative project that all family units complete. The process and the finished product are up to each individual family unit. Hence, families can be comfortable with not having to make a lot of choices, yet have the freedom to be creative in how to complete their project. Practically speaking, using only one project makes it much easier to gauge work time and to assemble your supplies and materials. Group spirit tends to remain higher as working on a single project helps enhance dialogue within families and between families.

The one exception I do make to this guideline is when I work specifically with a parent-teen group. The nature of adolescence, and its effect on the parent-child relationship, can sometimes create a threatening and stressful environment for families to work solely in individual family units. Therefore, in leading a parent-teen group in intergenerational learning I will often utilize a learning center approach to help maintain a lighter atmosphere.

As you direct families into the Discovery Time it would be helpful if you as a leader would provide a sample of a completed project to assist your families in understanding their assignment and to stimulate their creativity. This will assist you in explaining the directions for the activity as well as give your own family a chance to experience family discovery at home.

There is one more thing I would like to mention about your creative projects. While in the process of writing this book, I met with a good friend at the church to review part of the working manuscript. She raised an interesting point.

"The activities are all great," she said. "You have some really neat things here. But what do we do about the clutter at home? Do you realize how much stuff a family will have after it's all over!"

I must admit, she raised an issue I had not thought of before. What should families do with all this "stuff" they collect from an intergenerational learning series? The most obvious choice is, of course, they can keep it. And many families elect to do so, as a reminder of their experience together. In some sessions the projects are meant to be kept for follow-up within the home setting. The process of assimilating Bible truths into the home can be greatly assisted when we have a physical reminder of that which we have learned and experienced together.

But there is another simple answer to this question. That is, give it away! As the session or series draws to a close, suggest that those families who are so inclined give their various projects as gifts to another family or individual. They can give a gift to a family in their neighborhood, a relative, or take it to someone in a senior citizens' home. Even hospital patients, nursing home residents, or shut-ins are likely candidates for such a gift. You could even work with your pastor to organize a "visitation detail."

There are two benefits for the family that chooses to give its projects as gifts to someone else. First, giving projects away can become a creative way for a family to help others feel the touch of God's love. Giving the project to someone, with a simple explanation of what it is and what it means, can also be a safe and nonthreatening way to give witness to one's own faith in Jesus Christ.

Parents can teach their children volumes about ministering to others by joining together in an intentional act of giving.

A second benefit is family interaction. It is very difficult to give a gift to someone else as a family and not talk about it. Giving your projects away creates another forum for a family to once again draw together in informal conversation concerning faith-in-life issues. As Mom and Dad explain what they are going to do and why, as they once again discuss the meaning of the project, as they rehearse with their children what should be said, families will be doing something together that stimulates and nurtures the spiritual relationship of the family.

Guided Conversation. As families are completing their projects, you as leader should encourage families to discuss the meaning of the Bible story and its application to them personally. Unfortunately, we adults are not always adept in dialoguing about spiritual things in an informal family context. Therefore, as families break up to begin their work you can suggest one or two questions they can discuss as they complete their family projects.

This is called guided conversation. The guided conversation is not only important for family learning time, but it is also a simple tool to assist in family interaction. Try to discourage parents from talking across tables to other parents about the weather or the ball game. Encourage focused family conversation on the point and meaning of the project they are completing.

Part Four: Sharing Time

After the projects are completed families once again gather together for a time of sharing. Sing one or two songs. Then ask families to share their projects with the rest of the group. If quite a few families are involved, you may want to break up the project sharing with singing in order to avoid monotony of routine.

To further drive home the point of the Bible theme, follow up your sharing with a discussion exercise. Simple exercises like Bible verse scrambles, acrostics, listing, word games, circle response, a Bible rebus, are all good discussion exercises that can be done in a short period of time.

If time allows sing another song or two. Then conclude your time in prayer. Consider using some creative prayer exercises. For instance, join hands in a large circle and ask participants to offer short sentence prayers. You could break the group into clusters of two or three families to close in prayer together. Or, let individual family units close with their own prayertime. In this case encourage the children to lead in prayer. Families could be requested to write a few prayer requests on a card and trade it with another family. Each family can lift up the requests in a family prayertime, and then continue praying for these requests throughout the next week.

Part Five: Family Project

Technically, the Family Project is not part of the actual session. It can, nevertheless, be a very important part of your experience. So much of our teaching in the church is geared to drawing conclusions without giving methods for implementing those conclusions outside the classroom setting. But effective Christian Education should stimulate more than just academic response. It should challenge learners to focus the principles of God's Word toward specific actions for application.

The Family Project helps accomplish this. It moves learning from the classroom to the world by providing specific ideas for families to follow up what they have experienced in the session. Some projects are simple and are structured for the home-family context. Others are more outward in focus, requiring family members to look beyond themselves to others. These projects, then, can assist a family in its own spiritual nurture, as well as help members become involved in simple acts of ministry.

The directions for the Family Project should be given at the close of the session. You can do this orally or in writing. There is an obvious benefit in giving the project directions in writing. Families will not have to rely on their memories after the session is over. If you are running a multisession series, you may want to consider distributing a sheet with all the project assignments listed on it. While you should still remind the group of the project at the end of each session, each family will have a record of the projects for easy reference toward specific actions for application.

Another strength of the Family Project is to lift the level of group enthusiasm. In a multisession series you can allow time at the beginning of some of the sessions for family members to share what they have done with their project suggestion. Their excitement can generate excitement in others and be mutually encouraging for other families to follow through with the Family Projects in their own homes.

An Afterthought

While there are many formats for doing intergenerational learning, I believe that this particular format will allow you a great deal of flexibility and adaptability in most any setting in which you find yourself. Even so, the important thing about formatting your learning session is to know yourself and your purpose. Each of us has a particular style of leadership and teaching. We each have a different conception of our purpose in teaching. Hence, the way I structure a learning session will be different from the way you will structure the same session.

As you lead intergenerational learning sessions, let *your* style emerge. Then format your sessions accordingly. Use a format with which you feel most comfortable and that will help you achieve your purposes most effectively.

FIVE

A Word about
Risks and Failure

I would like to add one last word to help you keep things in perspective. Please, feel free to fail! Yes, it is always more comfortable to learn from the mistakes of others than it is your own. That does not mean, however, that you will never make any mistakes. Doing intergenerational learning is a learned art that comes through practice. As in anything else you will find yourself making mistakes. You may even lay the proverbial egg on occasion!

Any new venture involves risks. With risks come the possibility of failure. But remember, success or failure is determined by the interaction experienced between participants. It is not based on how you feel after it is all over. Give yourself time to learn and grow, especially if you have never done intergenerational learning before. In time, and after much practice, you will see yourself and your skills bloom and grow. Just let yourself enjoy the process!

Having said all of that, I would like to point out two factors that will directly contribute to the success of your intergenerational programming. As in any other venture there will be things that are within your control and things that are beyond your control. How you handle those things within your control and how you respond to those things outside your control will influence the success of your program, or even whether or not there *is* a program!

Factors within Your Control

Planning. Many good ideas are lost for lack of planning! Likewise, many good programs are sidetracked because the leader failed to think through all the details. I have often heard it said, "You either work to plan, or plan to work," and, "He who fails to plan, plans to fail." Wise words, indeed.

If you really want your intergenerational learning program to succeed, you will need to be a detail person. You will have to be able to take inventory of necessary resources. Equipment will need to be in working order. All of the necessary supplies must be there for each session. Good promotion is needed to stimulate interest. All of these details should be cared for if you intend to provide a positive experience for those in your intergenerational learning group.

Environment. While you cannot always control the kind of room available to you, or have all of the audiovisual equipment you want, you can control the atmosphere and environment of your learning setting. Once again, do not take this for granted! Just because everyone is eager to be there does not mean your learning setting will be warm and attractive.

Room atmosphere is a subtle yet powerful aspect of the learning process. Room decor, lighting, ventilation, and room temperature are all important considerations in creating an environment conducive to learning and interaction.

Cleanliness will also affect the learning environment. A room that is dirty, unkempt, and cluttered will have an adverse effect on your participants. It may also tell them that you as a leader are really not interested in providing the best possible learning experience for them.

So watch your environment. Make it the best you possibly can. Nothing is too good for those you will be leading in this exciting learning program.

Leadership. While you may not be tremendously experienced

in doing intergenerational learning, you will nevertheless provide the key to how the sessions progress and how comfortable your participants feel. You need to relax and have fun if you want your participants to relax and have fun. You need to feel comfortable if you want them to feel comfortable. Do everything you can to put your participants at ease. Laugh with them. Encourage and affirm them. Learn with them. Enjoy what you are doing. And they will respond by eager expectation of what is in store for them.

Communication. When you are leading a session, does what you say make any sense? Occasionally, when I do seminars or workshops, my wife will tell me that my directions during the group activities were not very clear, or that my discussion questions were too complex. She has helped me a great deal in fine-tuning my ability to give direction and guidance during group work times, or in asking and answering questions during discussion periods.

The instructions you give to your group need to be clear, brief, and understandable. When asking or answering questions you need to be simple and direct. Remember, they cannot read your mind. They have not read your session outline. Try writing out everything you want to say in a given session. Check your vocabulary. Are you using words that are too hard for children to understand? If necessary, practice what you want to say. Say it to someone else to see if it is understandable. If it is not understandable you may well undermine all you want to accomplish in your learning session.

Lack of communication creates confusion. Confusion will only result in discouragement, and discouragement will not make your learning time enjoyable or meaningful. If you want to succeed in doing intergenerational learning make sure you can communicate in a group setting involving a wide span of ages.

Loss of Enthusiasm. When a new program is started there is generally a high degree of enthusiasm. But as the novelty wears off, so also does our interest. In doing intergenerational learning you will have to be prepared for people losing their sense of excitement, especially if you are running an extended learning series. The result can be group lethargy, at best. At worst, it can mean declining attendance.

Loss of enthusiasm is a cause for concern, but it is not a

paralyzing problem. In fact, it can be easily overcome. First, you as leader need to maintain your own sense of excitement throughout the program. Many of your participants will take their cue from you. If you are apologetic, they will likely question the value of the activity. If you are bored, they too will soon become bored. Your example will help determine group spirit.

During a session if you feel group morale beginning to slip, change the pace of your presentation. Do something different. Try an action rhyme, sing a highly active song, or use a high-involvement story presentation. Or do anything that will help generate group energy!

Another consideration is the length of your series. Do not let your series drag. Try running a short series so it can end on a high note. If you run a long series, you run a greater risk of your participants losing interest. This is especially true if this is a new venture in your church. Remember, intergenerational programming is a supplement to your age-group program, not a substitute for it. Therefore, be careful not to let the length of your series exceed the attention span of your participants.

Monopolizing Behavior. When any group meets there is always a chance that someone will dominate discussion, or otherwise occupy center stage. The same is no less true in intergenerational learning settings. The older generations may tend to dominate discussion activities leaving children out. Or, some children may attempt to put themselves at the center of attention.

While this can be annoying, it is not overwhelming. The key is in how you lead the session and the expectations you communicate by your leadership style. If you allow individuals to monopolize discussion, they will. Let it become obvious that the purpose of your time together is for interaction across generational lines, not within generations. Be direct in asking for responses. Let different age groups offer responses to specific parts of your discussion activities. For instance, you could ask, "Can any of the first-graders answer this question for us?" This is a subtle yet positive way to encourage the greatest participation possible.

The same applies to attention-getting behavior from children. In a positive and firm way you should communicate the expectation of appropriate behavior. Encourage families to sit together, rather than children moving through the room at will. Ask parents to direct the activities of their children to ensure they are working together. Be sure to communicate to families that this is a family time, for their family to be involved together in an informal but structured learning time.

Factors Beyond Your Control

The previous areas should be well within your ability to control. There are a few things, however, that are outside your ability to control. Even so, an appropriate response on your part will minimize any negative effect these factors will have on your intergenerational learning program.

Equipment and Facility. While you can control your learning environment, you will not always have the most ideal room or equipment with which to work. That does not have to hamstring your program, however. If anything, you should look at it as an opportunity to stretch your thinking and abilities in leading intergenerational learning.

Do not let lack of equipment or less-than-ideal facilities discourage your efforts. Find ways to adapt. If your room is too small you can limit enrollment. If you do not have much audiovisual equipment you can rely on a chalkboard, newsprint taped to the wall, or a homemade flip chart. Do not be afraid to borrow equipment from another church. If you cannot locate or afford the materials for more elaborate story presentations, then go with what is simple. Even the old standbys such as a flannelgraph, picture story, or simply telling a story can be effective if presented well and enthusiastically.

The key in working with deficiencies in equipment or facility is your attitude and ability to see the potential within the parameters of your situation.

Resistance. There is always a risk that such a program will meet with resistance in your congregation. Some congregations are not interested in pursuing this type of learning program. The reasons may vary. It may not fit into the church's schedule. Or the medium age in the congregation is quite high and the need for such a program is not apparent. It may appear to some to be trite, simplistic, or nonsubstantive. Resistance can come when people do not understand your purpose or intentions. Many of us tend to be critical of those things we do not understand. And then some churches are resistant or suspicious of anything new or different!

Resistance is painful, especially if it involves something in which you have made a significant personal investment. In some cases there will be little or nothing you can do about it. But, again, you can take some positive steps to help diminish the effect of these dynamics.

Where you sense general resistance or suspicion, work with the church leadership. Make sure what you are doing has their full support. Be positive and patient with those who would be critical of such a program. Keep explaining and answering their questions. Respond to their doubts with kindness, gentleness, and enthusiasm. Share your vision with as many as possible on an informal basis. All of this can be very wearisome just to do something you believe is important. But, there is no reason to let other people's fears or doubts pop your bubble!

When we suspended our evening programming in our small midwestern church there were a few older members of the congregation who were not sure of what we were doing. But as they experienced the sessions and saw the value of interaction between families, their opinions changed. The enthusiasm of some of the younger families was infectious. We just kept encouraging them and loving them along the way. I am not sure all of them changed their minds, but at least we provided the best possible experience for them. And after all, that is what it is all about.

Another important factor in overcoming resistance is understanding — more specifically, understanding the reasons for people's hesitancy. Often you can take steps to alleviate people's discomfort if you know what makes them uncomfortable. If there are specific aspects of intergenerational learning that make people uncomfortable, then work at easing their discomfort. If you gently work at removing *reasons* for resistance you may well remove resistance altogether.

If there are too many questions and uneasy feelings at the idea, perhaps you should postpone your plans for a while until you have developed a greater base of understanding. Remember, if it is worth doing, it is worth doing well — not to mention doing it right! You would be better off to try again later rather than force the issue now.

In the meantime do not lose your vision. Try running a small group for young families for a limited period of time. Then invite another group of families together and do it again. While you may not be able to control the congregational attitude toward your vision, you can control your attitude toward them. There is always more than one way to fulfill a vision.

Family Dynamics. Another area over which you will have no control is the dynamics within the individual families that participate in your program. Families come in many shapes and varieties. Some families exude warmth and love. Communication lines are clear and unencumbered. Relationships are rich. Mutual affirmation is evident.

Other families, however, are not so privileged. Conversation comes hard. Relationships are complex and strained. Some of these families openly demonstrate hostility in the way they talk and work together. Some parents will not let their children do anything during the Family Discovery Time because they do not want them "messing anything up." Other parents will lead by yelling at or belittling their children. Sometimes the children are undisciplined or less than cooperative.

What can you do to assist a family that seems to be dysfunctional? Well, there is very little you can do to change their patterns of relating through a few intergenerational learning sessions. You can, however, do everything in your power to encourage, assist, and affirm them as they work together. Let them know you appreciate their presence at the sessions. Encourage the children. Shower compliments on them for their efforts. Tell them they are doing a great job. Tell the parents you like their approach to the project. Intentionally catch them working together and tell them you like the way they cooperate with each other to complete the project.

Again, while you cannot control what happens in a given family structure, you can control your response to each family. You can likewise take intentional steps to make their time together the best possible experience they could ever have in intergenerational learning.

Lack of Interest. Few things can deflate your ego as much as spending a great deal of time planning a session to which only a few come. But face it, just because we see and feel the need for intergenerational learning does not mean everyone else will! In fact, you may find that only a few families in your church will want to take time out of their schedules for such a venture.

Some parents, right or wrong, want to have a break from their children when they come to church. They sincerely desire to be nurtured as an adult for a while. On the other hand, older children, particularly teenagers, may not feel real comfortable participating with their parents in a learning series. Then, too, church leaders may not feel the need is intense enough to build such a program into the church's already busy schedule.

Everyone marches to the beat of a different drum. Creating interest in a program can be as much of a challenge as meeting people's needs through that same program. But that does not mean it cannot be done. It may just take longer than you would like. In the meantime, keep sharing informally with others about your ideas. Listen to what people say and find points of need to which intergenerational learning can relate. Gather a group of families together periodically for an evening of intergenerational learning. Creating positive experiences for people can sometimes prick their interest and help them see both the need and vision for something different.

Ages and Needs. As generations meet together for a learning session, there are many varying needs represented. Styles of learning differ with each age group. Each generation thinks, learns, and behaves differently.

Trying to meet the wide variety of needs present in an intergenerational context can be problematic. Planning activities that appeal to the wide span of ages is equally challenging. Moreover, communication can be a problem. Adults may tend to talk above the children, keeping themselves somewhat aloof. Or, they may overcompensate and speak down to the children, or act in ways that are somewhat childish.

Ironic, isn't it? The greatest asset of intergenerational learning can also be the biggest challenge. You cannot change that fact. If you did it would no longer be considered intergenerational learning! But, you can plan for it.

First, you can model appropriate communication skills. It is important that you as leader demonstrate ways of relating to children and adults in a mixed setting without neglecting one or the other. It is possible to speak simply without being simplistic. It is possible to appeal to the childlikeness in all of us without acting childish.

Secondly, plan your activities well. As stated previously, make sure your activities make allowances for the varying levels of ability of your participants. Continue to encourage older participants to assist the younger ones. Do all you can to keep people involved together. As they share together in positive ways the disparity of age and need will likely disappear.

One Last Word

Failing is a scary thing. But it is not the end of the world. When you do what you can to make sure everything is done well, and done right, then be content that you did the best you could. My mother practiced a very good habit. Whenever any of us kids did not think we did very well at something that was important to us, she would put her arms around us, or put her hand on our shoulder and say, "Well, kid, you did the best you could, and that's what matters most!" Tagging something a failure is really a subjective value judgment, isn't it?

Do the best you can. Be confident within yourself that the benefits outweigh the risks. Control those factors that are within your ability to control. Work creatively with those factors that seem outside your ability to control. And you will soon be on your way to being a great leader of intergenerational learning.

SIX

Curriculum for Intergenerational Learning
Celebrating God's Love
(A 13-week Program)

The following units of study are offered to help you get started in your program of intergenerational learning. They are reflective of the concerns and issues addressed in the previous chapters. The first program is a full 13-week unit, with all the supportive resources and materials you need to use it. The second and third programs are in outline form, offering suggested approaches and activities for each session.

These programs are not intended for continuing or consecutive usage. Each stands independently of the other. Neither is it necessary to gear the length of your series to the number of sessions in any of these units. If this is your first time, I would suggest that you start small. Perhaps run a single session, or a series of three to six sessions. As the concept of intergenerational learning gains positive momentum in your congregation, then branch out into other types of learning formats.

Plan your program wisely so as to avoid the feeling of redundancy. Plan for a variety of experiences. And as you plan remember, intergenerational learning experiences are not substitutes for other forms of church education. Rather, they are supplements to the overall Christian education and family nurture ministries of your church.

I trust these programs will provide a meaningful and rewarding experience of intergenerational learning for you and your church

Unit Title:	Celebrating God's Love
Scripture Focus:	Parables of Jesus, from Luke and Matthew
Unit Theme:	The parables are everyday stories that teach us the many ways God shows His love to us. This learning unit is designed to help participants gain new understanding and appreciation of the ways God's love reaches into our lives.
Age Group:	Age three and up

Unit Title:	Celebrating God's Love
Session:	1
Title:	The God Who Forgives
Scripture:	Luke 7:36-50; Matthew 18:23-25
Theme:	Because God loves us He willingly forgives us for our sins when we ask Him to, even though we don't deserve it. We then should forgive others.

A. Readiness Activity (As families arrive)

Name Tags. Using a half sheet of construction paper, instruct families to make name tags. Each member should write his or her first name, then draw a picture of something he or she enjoys doing. They should hang the tags around their necks with a piece of yarn. Encourage them to share their tags with each other.

Materials for Name Tags: Construction paper, yarn, markers, crayons, scissors, paper punches, instruction card, sample name tag.

B. Group Time (10–20 minutes)

Welcome. Gather the group together and welcome them to this first session of your unit. Introduce yourself and share your name tag with them. Then briefly introduce the unit theme.

To introduce the session theme, invite two older elementary-age children to come up to the front (without eyeglasses). Give them each a pillow.

Tell one child to hit the other with the pillow. Then ask the other child what he should do with his pillow in return. Your goal is to instigate a small pillow fight. After a few exchanges ask the children if hitting each other in return was a good idea. Then ask them why. After a very brief dialogue, tell the group, "We will be hearing a Bible story today that will tell us some important things about the way God wants us to treat other people, especially those who do things to us that we don't like."

Materials for Welcome: Two large bed pillows.

Singing: Sing several songs or choruses.

Materials for Singing: Chorus book.

Scripture Presentation. Present the Parable of the Two Debtors (Matthew 18:23-25), using simultaneous mime. Recruit several people to play the roles of the two servants, the king, and the king's jailers.

After the presentation break into family units for the Family Discovery Time. State that they will be working on a project to reinforce the truth that when God forgives us, He is doing a great thing for us. He is telling us that He will not ever hold all the bad things we have done against us. He promises to forget all about them. And He wants us to do the same for others who do things to us that may not be very nice.

Give instructions for the discovery activity.

Materials for Scripture Presentation: Bible, story script, actors.

C. Family Discovery Time (20–30 minutes)

Family Graffiti. Distribute a large sheet of newsprint to each family. Instruct members to draw a simulation of a brick wall and then add their own graffiti. Using phrases, Bible verses, pictures, and artwork, demonstrate the meaning of the parable.

List the following concepts on the chalkboard to give them assistance as they work: why God forgives us, what we should forgive others for, the benefits of forgiveness, and what forgiveness means.

Materials for Family Graffiti: Newsprint, crayons, markers,

magazines, glue, scissors, chalkboard, chalk, sample of completed project.

Guided Conversation. As families work on their projects encourage them to discuss the question, "Why does God forgive us?"

D. Sharing Time (15–20 minutes)

Singing: Call the group back together and sing one or two songs or choruses.

Materials for Singing: Chorus book.

Share Projects. Invite each family to show their graffiti to the entire group and explain.

Discussion Exercise. Do an acrostic on the word "Forgiven." Write the word on the chalkboard or sheet of newsprint, vertically (from top down). Have the group suggest words beginning with each letter in completing the sentence "Forgiveness is. . . ."

Wrap up by stating, "God has done a great thing in forgiving us. It really shows how much He loves us. We can help others experience that same love when we forgive them just like God has forgiven us." Challenge them to use the words they listed to show forgiveness to someone else during the next week.

Materials for Discussion Exercise: Chalkboard and chalk, or newsprint and marker.

Closing. Sing another song and close in prayer, thanking God for the wonderful gift of forgiveness He has given to us that we in turn can give to others.

Materials for Closing: Chorus book.

E. Family Project

Talk further about the words that were listed in the "Forgiveness is . . ." exercise. Each member of the family should say specifically how they will use some of those words to show God's forgiveness to someone who did something to them that was not very nice.

STORY SCRIPT: The Two Debtors (Matthew 18:23-35)
(Simultaneous Mime)

Once after Jesus taught His disciples about forgiveness, Peter asked Him, "Lord, how often do we need to forgive someone when he does something bad to us? Is seven times enough?"

Jesus said to Peter, "No! Not seven times, but 70 times 7!"

Well, Peter was really confused! So, to help him understand, Jesus told this story: "Once there was a great king in the land. He had great power, and could have whatever he wanted just by raising his hand. One day, he decided to have all his servants pay back all the money they had borrowed from him. So, he did.

"Soon he found that one servant owed him a million dollars. So he ordered his jailers to bring this man to him. The jailers went out to find the man. The jailers found the man and ordered him to come before the king. As the man came before the king, he bowed very low and asked, 'What can your servant do for you, Oh great and powerful king?'

"The king ordered the man to pay all of the money back. But the man was poor and said he could not possibly pay back all of that money. Well, the king became very angry. He raised his hand and ordered the servant, his wife, his children, and everything he owned to be sold to repay the debt.

"But the servant fell on his knees, begging and pleading with the king. 'Please, be patient with me, Oh great and mighty king!' he said. 'Surely, I will pay back everything! Just give me some time!'

"Well, the king was deeply moved by the servant's pleadings, and took pity on him. Raising his hand he said, 'I forgive your debt!' So the man got up and left the palace rejoicing.

"But on his way home the servant saw a fellow servant who owed him ten dollars. He ran over to his friend and grabbed him by the throat. He started shaking him and yelled at him, 'Pay back that ten dollars you owe me, or else!'

"Very frightened, his fellow servant fell to the ground and begged for mercy. 'Please be patient with me! Surely, I will pay back everything! Just give me some time!' But he refused to listen to him. Instead, he called the jailers to come and throw the man in prison until he could pay back every cent.

"When word got back to the king, he became very angry. Raising his hand, he ordered the jailers to bring the man to him. The man came before the king, and bowed very low, almost touching the ground. The king glared at the servant. He shook his finger at him and shouted, 'You wicked servant. I cancelled your debt because you begged me to. You should have had mercy on your fellow servant just like I did you. But because you didn't, I'm going to turn you over to the jailers to be thrown in prison until you pay back every bit of what you owe me.'

"With that, the jailers grabbed the servant, and dragged him off to prison kicking and screaming."

Unit Title: Celebrating God's Love
Session: 2
Title: The God Who Speaks
Scripture: Luke 8:4-15
Theme: God shows His love for us by giving us His Word. Through it we can know how He wants us to live.

A. Readiness Activity (As families arrive)

Mural. Tape a long sheet of newsprint on the wall with a lettered heading "Growing with God's Word." Draw a picture of a flower garden, showing a row of several flowers without petals. Cut out large flower petals from construction paper, one for each participant. As families arrive, instruct them to write verses from Psalm 119 on the flower petals and tape them to the flowers on the mural.

Materials for Mural: Newsprint with mural background, construction-paper flower petals, markers, crayons, tape, instruction card, several Bibles open to Psalm 119, sample of completed flower petal.

B. Group Time (10–20 minutes)

Welcome. Gather the group together and welcome them to the session. Introduce the session theme by holding up two plants, one dried and wilted, and one green and healthy. Ask the group, "If you were a plant, which one of these would you like to be? Why?" After a few answers are given, state that today they will be hearing a Bible story about plants that will teach some very important truths about how we can be like the healthy plant.

Materials for Welcome: A healthy plant, a dried and wilted plant.

Singing. Sing several songs or choruses

Materials for Singing: Chorus book.

Scripture Presentation. Present the Parable of the Sower (Luke 8:9-15) with the overhead projector story "Sower," from Bill Hovey Visuals (see resource listing in back of book).

After the presentation break into family units for the discovery project. State that they will be working on a project to reinforce the truth from the story that God's Word is important for us. When we do what it says, we show God that we are His friend and we make Him happy. Give instructions for the discovery activity.

Materials for Scripture Presentation: Bible, overhead projector, story transparencies, projection screen, extension cord.

C. Family Discovery Time (20–30 minutes)

Family Promise Book. Distribute a pack of 5″x7″ index cards, or half sheets of construction paper to each family. Instruct them to make a Family Promise Book by printing selected Bible verses on the cards, punching two holes in the side of the stack, and binding it together with pieces of yarn. A cover can be made from poster board, construction paper, or wallpaper samples and decorated. The book can be laid out on a coffee table at home with a different verse showing each day. Encourage each family to choose one verse to recite or read as a family during the Sharing Time.

(Note to the leader: In the event you have families attending with little or no knowledge of Bible promises or verses, you may want to provide a list of Bible references for all families to use in completing the project. You should also make available several copies of a simple paraphrase or translation from which they can copy. This will help avoid unnecessary embarrassment and also save time for families as they make their books.)

Materials for Family Promise Book: 5″x7″ cards or half sheets of construction paper, wallpaper samples, poster board, scissors, paper punches, yarn, markers, crayons, sample of completed project.

Guided Conversation. As families work on choosing their verses for the sharing time, encourage them to discuss the question, "What does this verse mean?"

D. Sharing Time (15–20 minutes)

Singing. Call the group back together and sing one or two songs or choruses.

Materials for singing: Chorus book.

Sharing Projects. Ask families to volunteer to read or recite the verse they chose during the activity time.

Discussion Exercise. Using Psalm 19:8, make a verse scramble game. Print the verse on poster board, including the reference.

Cut out each word and tape the cards to a chalkboard in a scrambled order. Put the cards in the right order as the group works to unscramble them.

Wrap up by saying, "God's Word is an important part of our lives as His children. It teaches us how to live in a way that makes God happy. We should desire it, just like we would desire to eat the best dessert at mealtime! Because when we do what God's Word tells us to do, we will grow closer to God and become healthy Christians." Challenge them to make Bible reading a part of their daily routine.

Materials for Discussion Exercise: Verse word cards, masking tape or tacks, chalkboard or bulletin board.

Closing. Sing one more song and close in prayer, thanking God for giving us His Word by which to live, and asking for His help in obeying it.

Materials for Closing: Chorus book.

E. Family Project

Memorize three verses this week from your "Family Promise Book." Be sure to review each verse before going on to the next one. Discuss the meaning of each one after you've memorized it.

FAMILIES GROWING TOGETHER

Unit Title:	Celebrating God's Love
Session:	3
Title:	The God Who Reaches
Scripture:	Luke 10:25-37
Theme:	God's love is shown to others when we who have experienced it reach out to help others who are in need.

A. Readiness Activity (As families arrive)

Buttonhole Flower. Instruct families to make buttonhole flowers using construction paper and pipe cleaners. Precut small flowers from construction paper, one for each participant. As families arrive, have them each color a flower, bend a loop in the end of a pipe cleaner, and tape the flower to the loop. Direct families to give their flowers to someone else in the group.

Materials: Construction paper, markers, crayons, pipe cleaners, scissors, masking tape, instruction card, sample flower.

B. Group Time (10–20 minutes)

Welcome. Gather the group together and welcome them to the session. Introduce the session by having everyone stand up, touch another person, and in unison say loudly, "God loves you, I love you, and that's the way it should be!" Then touch someone else and do the same thing. Do this three times.

Explain that what they just did was to reach out to someone else and share God's love with them, just like they did when they gave their flowers away. State that today they will hear a Bible story about how to show others how much God loves them.

Singing. Sing several songs or choruses.

Materials for Singing: Chorus book.

Scripture Presentation. Present the Parable of the Good Samaritan (Luke 10:25-37) using puppets. Recruit several teens or adults as puppeteers. Use the Arch Book cassette tape "The Good Samaritan" as your story resource. Have the puppets act out the story as the cassette narrates it. Be sure your tape player is in a location to be easily heard by both puppeteers and audience. If possible, recruit your helpers the week before so they can practice with the tape.

After the presentation, break into family units for the discovery project. State that they will be working on a project to reinforce the truth that God reaches out to love others through us when we help other people who are having problems. Give instructions for the discovery activity.

Materials for Scripture Presentation: Bible, puppets, stage, Arch Book cassette, recorder, extension cord, puppeteers.

C. Family Discovery Time (20–30 minutes)

Doorknob Card. Have each family make a doorknob card that they can share with someone else. Instruct them to cut their cards out of construction paper, and put a message of hope and encouragement for someone who needs to know God's love in their life circumstances. Laminate the completed card with clear Con-Tact Paper. They should discuss who will receive each card they make.

Materials for Doorknob Card: Construction paper, magazines, glue, scissors, markers, crayons, clear Con-Tact Paper, sample of completed project.

Guided Conversation. As families work on their projects encourage them to discuss the question, "How did the Good Samaritan show God's love to the wounded traveler?"

D. Sharing Time (15–20 minutes)

Singing. Call the group back together and sing one or two songs or choruses.

Materials for Singing: Chorus book.

Sharing Projects. Invite each family to share their doorknob cards with the rest of the group, stating to whom they will be giving them.

Discussion Exercise. Letter the heading "Sensing the Need" on a large sheet of newsprint. Draw pictures representing the five senses; i.e., hand, nose, mouth, ear, eye. State that the Good Samaritan showed God's love to the wounded traveler by helping him when he had a real problem. Point to the pictures of the five senses. Ask the group to give you words or phrases for each of the senses in answer to the question, "How can we use our senses to show loving actions to someone who is having problems?"

Some possible answers are: Hand — touching others, physical

support, helping hand, comforting arm; Nose — "nosey" enough to help, follow your nose, "nose" where the problems are, "smells" trouble; Mouth — offering a kind word, giving encouragement; Ear — sympathetic ear, listening, hearing what's spoken, hearing the pain; Eye — seeing the need, looking for trouble, recognizing others' difficulties.

Wrap up by saying, "Those of us who have experienced God's love in our own lives can help others know God's love when we help them. No matter what kind of help we give, God is always pleased when His children help others who are having problems." Challenge the group to use the ways they listed to show God's love to someone else during the next week.

Materials for Discussion Exercise: Newsprint with pictures and heading, marker, masking tape or tacks, chalkboard or bulletin board.

Closing. Sing one more song and close in prayer, thanking God for the opportunities He gives us for sharing His love with others. Pray that we will be faithful in that trust.

Materials for Closing: Chorus book.

E. Family Project

Discuss to whom you will be giving your Doorknob Cards and why. Talk about what else you can do to help each one of these persons. Pray for each one and then make an appointment to visit them during the week.

Unit Title: Celebrating God's Love
Session: 4
Title: The God Who Hears
Scripture: Luke 11:5-8
Theme: Because God loves us so much, He wants us to talk to Him and eagerly listens to us when we pray.

A. Readiness Activity (As families arrive)

Praise Chain. Cut out strips of construction paper for families to make a chain when they arrive. Instruct them to write an item of praise on several construction paper strips, and staple them together as links in a chain. Provide a short starter chain for families to staple their paper links to so as to create one long chain.

Materials for Praise Chain: Construction paper strips, markers, crayons, staplers, staples, starter chain, instruction card.

B. Group Time (10–20 minutes)

Welcome. Gather the group together and welcome them to the session. Introduce the session theme by holding up a telephone made from two tin cans and a long piece of string. Have two children come up and demonstrate how it works by having one child "call" the other and ask to borrow a favorite toy. State that God loves us so much He wants us to talk to Him. Explain that they will hear a Bible story today that will teach an important truth about talking to God.

Materials for Welcome: Tin can telephone.

Singing. Sing several songs or choruses.

Materials for Singing: Chorus book.

Scripture Presentation. Present the Parable of the Midnight Friend (Luke 11:5-8) in the form of a skit. Recruit some adults to help you. After the skit state that the Bible story teaches us an important truth about the need to keep praying and not give up. God loves us so much He wants us to talk to Him. He listens to us when we do. But the Bible also speaks of other kinds of prayer. Using an overhead transparency, explain that the Bible speaks of various kinds of prayer: Praise and Thanksgiving (for who God is and what He does), Confession (for forgiveness of sin), Petition (asking for what is needed), and

Intercession (on behalf of someone else).

After the presentation break into family units for the discovery project. State that they will be working on a project to reinforce the truth that God eagerly wants to hear us when we pray. Give instructions for the discovery activity.

Materials for Scripture Presentation: Bible, script, actors, premade overhead transparency, overhead projector, projection screen, extension cord.

C. Family Discovery Time (20–30 minutes)

Circle of Prayer. Give each family unit four tin cans. Have them decorate each can for the specific types of prayer just mentioned; i.e., one can for praise and thanksgiving, one can for petition, one can for confession, and one can for intercession. Be sure each can is labeled. After decorating and labeling each can, tape them together by putting masking tape on the top edges and across the bottom.

Materials for Circle of Prayer: large tin cans, glue, construction paper, masking tape, scissors, markers, crayons, magazines, sample of completed project.

Guided Conversation. Provide strips of construction paper for families. As they complete their cluster of cans, ask them to write down prayer items on the paper strips and place them in the appropriate can.

Materials for Guided Conversation: Construction paper strips, pens or pencils.

D. Sharing Time (15–20 minutes)

Singing. Call the group back together and sing one or two songs or choruses.

Materials for Singing: Chorus book.

Sharing Projects. Invite families to show their "Circle of Prayer," sharing with the group any item of praise, thanksgiving, or request they placed in their cluster of cans. Remember these during the closing prayer time.

Wrap up your sharing time by saying, "God loves us so much He wants us to talk to Him. Like the tin can phone, we have a direct line to God to talk to Him whenever we want. And we should do it as much as we can, and not give up. Just like you enjoy getting a telephone call, God always wants us to talk to

Him. He eagerly listens to us when we come to Him in prayer." Encourage them to leave their "Circle" someplace at home, along with strips of paper, for family members to write down prayer items during the day and place them in the cans. Challenge them to spend time daily as a family reviewing their prayers together.

Closing. Sing a chorus to lead into a group prayer experience. Then break into smaller groups. Give each group a section of the "Praise Chain" made during the Readiness Activity. Direct them to offer sentence prayers of praise using their chain length. Then form a large circle, join hands, and challenge the group to remember any specific requests given during the Sharing Time throughout the next week. Conclude by singing the Doxology together.

Materials for Closing: Praise Chain, chorus book.

E. Family Project

Make it a practice to sit down together once a week for a special family prayer time using your Circle of Prayer and slips of paper.

STORY SCRIPT: The Midnight Friend (Luke 11:5-8)
(Skit)

1: Once when Jesus had been praying, one of His disciples came to Him and said, "Lord, teach us a prayer that we can say, just like John the Baptist taught his friends." So, Jesus taught His disciples the Lord's Prayer.

   Then, wanting to teach them more about prayer, He used this illustration. Suppose an old friend of yours came to visit you. He had traveled to your home from a long distance. What would you do?

2: (Knocks on door) Hey, Joshua! Open up. It's Samuel.

3: (Opens door — greets friend with hand shake and hug) Samuel! It's really you. Come in, come in. Let me make you something to eat. You must have been traveling all day and all night just to get here.

1: But when Joshua looked in his cupboard, all the bread was gone. So he went next door to his friend's house. The only problem was it was midnight! So, what do you suppose he did?

3: (Pounds on door several times) Hey, Jacob! (Knocks again)

4: (Awakened from sleep—groans) What time is it? Who's there?

3: (Pounds on door and shouts) Hey Jake! Open up, it's me, Joshua! A friend of mine just arrived for a visit and I don't have any bread to feed him. I need to borrow three loaves of bread.

4: (Angrily) What's the matter with you! It's midnight. Don't ask me to get up. The door is locked for the night and we are all in bed. I can't help you! Go home!

3: C'mon Jake, I need your help! Just three loaves. That's all I ask.

4: (Gets up—is very disgusted) OK! OK! I'll do it this time, but don't expect it to happen again. (Pretends to get bread out of cupboard; goes to door and gives to friend) Good night!

3: Thanks man! I knew you'd come through!

1: And that's what your neighbor will do for you, too! If you keep knocking long enough, he will get up and give you everything you want, just because you keep knocking. And so it is with prayer. Keep on asking and you will keep on getting. Keep on looking and you will keep on finding. Knock and the door will be opened. Everyone who asks, receives. All who seek, find. And the door is opened to everyone who knocks.

Unit Title: Celebrating God's Love
Session: 5
Title: The God Who Gives True Wealth
Scripture: Luke 12:13-21
Theme: In His great love God has provided for us, giving us all that we have. He therefore wants us to use what He has given us to serve Him.

A. Readiness Activity (As families arrive)

Bulletin Board. Letter a heading on a bulletin board "We Give Thee But Thine Own." In the middle of the bulletin board put a figure of a large offering plate being held by a pair of hands. Provide precut pieces of green construction paper, about the size of a dollar bill. As families arrive instruct them to make "dollar bills" out of construction-paper pieces and staple them in place in the offering plate.

Materials for Bulletin Board: Precut green construction-paper pieces, scissors, markers, crayons, staplers, instruction card, sample dollar bills.

B. Group Time (10–20 minutes)

Welcome. Gather the group together and welcome them to the session. Introduce the session theme by pulling a large balloon from your pocket. Blow up the balloon until it is completely full of air. Ask, "What will happen if I try to put more air in this balloon than it can hold?" After several respond, continue blowing up the balloon until it pops. State that today they will hear a story Jesus told about a man who wanted more money than he could ever keep or spend. He kept it all to himself and didn't share it with anyone. He didn't pop, but he learned a very important lesson.

Materials for Welcome: Large balloon.

Singing. Sing several songs or choruses.

Materials for Singing: Chorus book.

Scripture Presentation. Present the Parable of the Rich Fool (Luke 12:13-21) using the filmstrip "Jesus Teaches About God's Care" from Bible Story Filmstrips (produced by Gospel Light Publications). Have several copies of the script ready and recruit people to read the parts of the various characters in the story.

After the filmstrip break into family units for the discovery project. State that they will be working on a project to reinforce the truth from the story that God has given us many things. All that we have belongs to Him. So we should use everything we have for His service. Give instructions for the discovery activity.

Materials for Scripture Presentation: Bible, filmstrip, filmstrip projector, copies of script, projection screen, extension cord.

C. Family Discovery Time (20–30 minutes)

Giving Mobile. Direct each family to make a Giving Mobile. Distribute two wire clothes hangers or one-quarter-inch wood dowels to each family. Instruct them to make a mobile displaying the many different ways we can use the things we have to serve God.

Materials for Giving Mobile: Wire clothes hangers or one-quarter-inch wood dowel rods, yarn, construction paper, magazines, glue, crayons, markers, scissors, paper punches, sample of completed project

Guided Conversation. As families work encourage them to discuss the question, "What does God want us to do with our money? Why?" Discuss various ways to give as you make your mobile.

D. Sharing Time (15–20 minutes)

Singing. Call the group back together and sing one or two songs or choruses.

Materials for Singing: Chorus book.

Sharing Projects. Ask for families to volunteer to share their Giving Mobile with the group.

Discussion Exercise. Determine a code for the alphabet (numbers, letters, symbols, etc.). Write Proverbs 11:25 on newsprint using your code. Hang the newsprint on the chalkboard or the wall. Next to the coded verse, hang your code key for easy reference. Have children come up and cross out the coded letters to write in the correct letter, e.g., "Look, here's a number 5. What letter does number 5 represent? That's right! Who can come up and cross out all of the 5's and write the letter 'd'?" When the verse is decoded say it together as a group.

Wrap up by saying, "God has given us so much. Every time God gives something to us, we have the opportunity to use it to serve Him. We can serve Him by giving generously in the many ways we have shown on our Giving Mobiles. If God has given everything we have so freely, then we should use it to serve Him as a way of saying thank you to God!"

Materials for Discussion Exercise: Coded verse and code on newsprint, marker, masking tape or tacks, chalkboard or bulletin board.

Closing. Sing one more song and close in prayer, thanking God for all He has given to us, and asking Him to help us be faithful in using these gifts for His service.

Materials for Closing: Chorus book.

E. Family Project

Before the next Sunday, discuss what each family member can give in the offering during Sunday School or the worship service. Talk about how your money helps the church do God's work. Then prepare your offerings to be given the following Sunday.

Unit Title: Celebrating God's Love
Session: 6
Title: The God Who Takes Us Home
Scripture: Luke 12:35-38; Matthew 25:1-13
Theme: God loves us so much He will someday send Jesus to come and take us to heaven to live with Him forever.

A. Readiness Activity (As families arrive)

Door Decoration. On the door of your meeting room, make a scene background that depicts heaven; e.g., light-blue backdrop, golden throne, white clouds, yellow or gold rays of light, etc. Precut two or three patterns of angels from construction paper, one for each participant. As families arrive instruct them to fill in the details on an angel (color the face, gown, etc.) and tape it to the door scene. There should be one angel figure for each family member present. Note: If your meeting room does not have a door, you can do the same activity as a wall mural or bulletin board.

Materials for Door Decoration: Precut construction-paper angels, markers, crayons, scissors, Scotch Tape, sample of finished angel, instruction card.

B. Group Time (10–20 minutes)

Welcome. Gather the group together and welcome them to the session. Introduce the session theme by asking four or five women to come up and pantomime a specific activity they might do to get the house ready to receive a special guest. For added fun, ask them to do it in a frantic state. Let the rest of the group guess what each one is doing. State that today they will be looking at a Bible story about what we need to do to be prepared to receive a very special guest when He comes to see us.

Singing. Sing several songs or choruses.

Materials for Singing: Chorus book.

Scripture Presentation. Present the Parable of the Ten Young Women (Matthew 25:1-13) by doing a group story. Choose several people to play the parts of the ten young women, the bridegroom, and the wedding party. As you tell the story, instruct the participants to act it out, including sound effects, as the story line directs.

After the presentation, break into family units for the discovery activity. State that they will be working on a project to reinforce the truth from the story that God loves us so much that someday He will send Jesus back to take all of His children to heaven to live with Him forever. But until that time God wants us to obey Him so we can be ready to go home with Jesus when He comes for us. If we are ready when He comes, we will be glad and happy to see Him. Give instructions for the discovery activity.

Materials for Scripture Presentation: Bible, story script, actors.

C. Family Discovery Time (20–30 minutes)

Family Coat of Arms. Provide each family with a large sheet of poster board to make a Family Coat of Arms. They should draw a large shield divided into four sections. A swath of ribbon should be drawn along the top and bottom of the shield. The top ribbon should show their name. Using art work and magazine pictures in each section of the shield they should put a scene of ways their family can prepare to be ready for the Lord when He returns; e.g., helping someone, going to church, reading the Bible, praying, etc. In the ribbon at the bottom instruct them to write a "family motto" which summarizes the meaning of the Bible story.

Materials for Coat of Arms: Poster board, crayons, markers, magazines, glue, scissors, sample of completed project.

Guided Conversation. As families work encourage them to discuss the question, "Are there any things missing on our Coat of Arms that we can do to help us be ready for Jesus when He comes for us?"

D. Sharing Time (15–20 minutes)

Singing. Call the group back together and sing one or two songs or choruses.

Materials for Singing: Chorus book.

Sharing Projects. Have each family voluntarily show and explain its Coat of Arms.

Discussion Exercise. Do a picture study. On poster board, mount several pictures from magazines of people doing various things, good and bad. Show each picture and have the group answer the question, "Are the people in this picture doing something that will make them ready for Jesus to come? Why or why not?" Post them on the chalkboard or bulletin board as you show each one.

Wrap up by saying, "It will be a great day when Jesus comes to take us home to live in heaven with Him. But until that time comes He wants us to be ready. First we need to give our lives to Jesus as our personal Saviour. Then we need to do the kinds of things you put on your Family Coat of Arms to help us be ready when Jesus comes back." Encourage them to hang their Coat of Arms somewhere conspicuous at home to remind them to be ready.

Materials for Discussion Exercise: Pictures mounted on poster board, masking tape or tacks, chalkboard or bulletin board.

Closing. Sing one more song and close in prayer, thanking God that someday Jesus will return to take us to live with Him forever. Pray that we will always do those things that will make us ready to go with Jesus when He comes for us.

Materials for Closing: Chorus book.

E. Family Project

Talk about some things that are not on your Coat of Arms, but that will help you be ready to meet Jesus when He returns. Choose one of these things on your Coat of Arms, or that you just discussed, and make special plans to do it as a family in the next week.

STORY SCRIPT: The Ten Young Women (Matthew 25:1-13) (Group Story)

One day, when Jesus was sitting on the Mount of Olives, the disciples came to Him and asked Him to tell them about when the world would end. Jesus told them many things about when the end would come. Then He told them this story about God's kingdom.

When God's kingdom finally comes, and Jesus returns from heaven, it will be like ten young women getting ready for a wedding celebration. With great care they took their lamps and went out to meet the bridegroom. Five of them were very smart. But the other five were very foolish.

The foolish ones took their lamps, but didn't bother to take any oil with them. The five who were wise, remembered to take some extra jars of oil with them. So they went, the wise young women carrying both their lamps and jars of oil, and the foolish ones carrying only their lamps.

It seemed like forever before the bridegroom came. It was so long in fact that they all became very tired and fell asleep. They all snored very loudly.

At midnight, they were awakened with a cry, "Here's the bridegroom! Come out to meet him!" Far off they could hear the great sound of a celebration. A great crowd of people was following the bridegroom down the road, singing and cheering and making all kinds of joyful sound.

Well, the young women all woke up. The five wise women put oil in their lamps and lit them. But the five foolish women didn't have any oil. So when they tried to light their lamps, they wouldn't light. Oh, they were frantic! "Oh no!" they exclaimed. Turning to the five wise women they said, "Please give us some oil for our lamps, too!"

But the five wise women shook their heads vigorously and said, "No!" They all shook their fingers and said, "There isn't enough for all of us. You'll just have to go into town and buy some for yourselves!"

So, they hurried off. But while they were going, the bridegroom and all those with him came by. The women who were ready went in with him to the wedding banquet. There were great sounds of rejoicing. And the door was shut tight.

Later, the other five women came, too. They could hear all the noise coming from inside. They pounded on the door very loudly and said, "Please, Sir. Open the door for us too!"

But the bridegroom shook his head and shouted back, "Why should I open the door for someone I don't even know!" The five foolish women went away very sad, while everyone at the feast continued to celebrate with great sounds of joy.

Jesus then said to His disciples, "Be sure you keep watch and are ready for Me when I come back because you surely will not know when that time will be."

    Unit Title: Celebrating God's Love
        Session: 7
          Title: The God Who Works in the World
    Scripture: Luke 13:18-21
       Theme: God loves the world and wants all people to become part of the family. So He uses us to help others experience His love and become part of His family.

A. Readiness Activity (As families arrive)

Smiley Face Medallions. Instruct families to make a smiley face medallion from yellow construction paper. They can punch a hole in their medallion for a piece of yarn to hang it around someone's neck. Have them share the joy of God's love by giving their medallion to someone else.

Materials for Medallions: Yellow construction paper, yarn, markers, crayons, paper punches, scissors, instruction card, sample medallion.

B. Group Time (10–20 minutes)

Welcome. Call the group together and welcome them to the session. Introduce the session theme by showing the group a lump of bread dough. As they watch mix some yeast with the dough and put the lump in a bread pan. Set the dough aside and tell the group you will look at it a little later to see what has happened. Then ask, "What does yeast do to bread dough?" After someone answers, state that today they will hear a Bible story that teaches an important lesson about how God wants His family to grow, and He wants us to help Him make it grow.

(Note to the leader: After you have introduced the session theme, have someone take the bread dough and put it into an oven in the church kitchen to bake. You will need to use a bread recipe that fully bakes within an hour. As you get ready to wrap up the session, bring the pan of bread back to show the change in size. After the session, slice the bread and give everyone a piece as a special treat.)

Materials for Welcome: Bread dough, yeast, bread pan.

Singing. Sing several songs or choruses.

Materials for Singing: Chorus book.

Scripture Presentation. Present the Parable of the Mustard

Seed and Yeast (Luke 13:18-21) using simultaneous mime. You will need volunteers to play the parts of the mustard seed/tree, birds, woman, lump of dough.

After the presentation, break into family units for the discovery activity. State that they will be working on a project to reinforce the truth from the story that God wants His family to get bigger, just like a small seed that grows into a big tree, or the way yeast makes a lump of dough get bigger. He wants all people to experience His love. And He wants to use us to help others become part of His family.

Materials for Scripture Presentation: Bible, story script.

C. Family Discovery Time (20–30 minutes)

Collage. Using poster board and magazines have each family make a collage of the many ways God works in the world to help people become part of His family. Instruct them to first draw a tree trunk or a loaf of bread; place the pictures either as leaves on the tree, or within the outline of the bread. Suggest they add a caption somewhere on the collage.

Materials for Collage: Poster board, magazines, markers, crayons, scissors, glue, sample of completed project.

Guided Conversation. As families work encourage them to discuss the question, "How can we help other people become part of God's family?"

D. Sharing Time (15–20 minutes)

Singing. Call the group back together and sing one or two songs or choruses.

Materials for Singing: Chorus book.

Sharing Projects. Have each family voluntarily show their collage.

Discussion Exercise. Do a pantomime game to reinforce the meaning of the parable. As families show their collages, have one or more family members act out a response to the question, "How can we help God make His family get bigger?" The rest of the group then guesses what the person(s) is doing.

Wrap up by showing how the bread has gotten bigger. Say to the group, "There are so many ways we can help God's family grow. And since we already know God's love, we should joyfully help others know that same love too! God wants all people to become His children. He wants His family to get bigger, just like our lump of bread dough. Let's use the ideas on our collages to help someone we know become part of God's family."

Closing. Sing one more song and close in prayer, thanking God for the opportunity He has given us to be involved in helping His family grow bigger. Pray that we will be faithful in that task.

Materials for Closing: Chorus book.

E. Family Project

Choose an elderly person in your community for whom you can volunteer to do some simple household chores; e.g., vacuuming, washing windows or floors, cleaning the kitchen or bathroom, yard work, etc.

STORY SCRIPT: The Mustard Seed and the Yeast (Luke 13:18-21; Matthew 13:31-33)
(Simultaneous Mime)

One day while Jesus was teaching, He saw that all the people were enjoying the wonderful things He was saying and doing. So He turned to them and asked, "What is the kingdom of God like?" Then He told these stories.

The kingdom of God is like a mustard seed. As a man goes out to plant his garden, he takes the mustard seed out of his bag with great care, for it is the smallest of all the seeds. Carefully he plants the seed in the ground. Then, as he gives the seed food and water, it grows up to be the biggest plant in the garden. In fact, it becomes a tree, and spreads out its branches. As the birds fly over the garden, they see the great branches of the tree. So they come down and perch in the tree.

The kingdom of God is also like yeast. Think of how a woman makes dough to bake her bread. She takes a small bit of yeast from a jar and puts it in the pile of flour. She mixes it all up. Finally, the yeast is spread through the whole pile until the flour grows into a great lump of dough.

This is what the kingdom of God is like. It starts out very small. But people see that God wants them to become part of His family. So one by one, people accept Jesus as Lord and Saviour. And slowly, God's family keeps getting bigger!

Unit Title: Celebrating God's Love
Session: 8
Title: The God Who Exalts
Scripture: Luke 18:9-14
Theme: Because of His love, God blesses us when we show true humility in the way we live.

A. Readiness Activity (As families arrive)

Crown of Life. Precut a pattern of a crown from construction paper, one for each participant. As families arrive instruct them to decorate their crowns, staple them together, and wear them.

Materials for Crown: Crown pattern precut from construction paper, markers, crayons, staplers, staples, instruction card, sample of completed crown.

B. Group Time (10–20 minutes)

Welcome. Gather the group together and welcome them to the session. Introduce the session theme by showing a large spring. Ask, "What will happen if I push down on this spring?" After the answer is given, push down on the spring and let it jump into the air. State that the only way a spring can go up is if it is first pushed down. Today they will hear a Bible story that teaches the important truth that the way to be blessed by God is to be humble and not act more important than others.

Materials for Welcome: Large spring.

Singing. Sing several songs or choruses.

Materials for Singing: Chorus book.

Scripture Presentation. Present the Parable of the Pharisee and the Tax Collector (Luke 18:9-14) using a skit. Recruit several people to play the parts of the Pharisee, Tax Collector, and Narrator before the session begins, and give them each a copy of the script. After the skit, break into family units for the discovery project. State that they will be working on a project to reinforce the truth from the story that some people act like they are better than other people. But God is happy when we don't act proud, or selfish, or treat people in bad ways. Give instructions for the discovery activity.

Materials for Scripture Presentation: Bible, skit script, actors.

C. Family Discovery Time (20–30 minutes)

Family Story. Instruct families to make finger, stick, clothes pin, paper plate, or paper sack puppets and write a simple everyday story to act out. The story should focus on one person willingly serving someone else and not being selfish. They will then present their stories in the Sharing Time.

Materials for Family Story: Tongue depressors, popsicle sticks, paper lunch sacks, paper plates, construction paper, crayons, markers, felt, yarn, scissors, glue, tape, sample of each kind of puppet.

Guided Conversation. As families develop their stories, encourage them to discuss together, "How do people act when they aren't humble?"

Sharing Time (15–20 minutes)

Singing. Call the group back together and sing one or two songs or choruses.

Materials for Singing: Chorus book.

Sharing Projects. Ask families to volunteer to share their puppet stories with the group. Sing a short song or two halfway through to help keep the sharing fresh.

Wrap up by saying, "When we are proud, we can act selfishly, or act better than someone else, or we treat people in bad ways. But God wants us to be humble. When we are humble, then we'll see others are just as good as we are and do good things for them. And God will bless us for it!"

Closing. Before singing a closing chorus, state that an important way we can learn humility is to worship God. Put a picture of Jesus in front of the room on a chair. Sing a worship chorus in closing. As you sing have the group bring their crowns up and lay them in front of the picture of Jesus, as a symbolic giving of themselves in worship to Him. Gather in a large circle and close in prayer, thanking God that He promises to bless us if we will humble ourselves before Him.

Materials for Closing: Chorus book, chair, picture of Jesus, crowns from Readiness Activity.

E. Family Project

Talk together about how other people in your community may not have as much as you do. Let your children even suggest names of children with whom they go to school that fall into this category. Discuss what you can do to be their friend. Then make an appointment to go to a nearby rescue mission or thrift shop and volunteer a few hours to help in whatever way may be needed.

STORY SCRIPT: The Pharisee and the Publican (Luke 8:9-14) (Skit)

1: (Enter Jesus) One day Jesus noticed that some of the people were very proud. They thought they were very holy, and looked down on everyone else around them. He did not look very happy about this. So, He told the people this story.

2: Once there was a Pharisee (enter Pharisee). He came into the temple one day to pray. He was very proud. And he walked in very tall. Seeing that the people were all very impressed with his appearance, he was very pleased.

But then a tax collector came into the temple to pray. Nobody liked tax collectors. They were considered terrible people (enter tax collector). As he came into the temple he saw how everyone scoffed at him. He felt very alone. Quietly, with his head down, without pretense, he stood off to the side of the temple, trying to hide behind a pillar.

The Pharisee, looking at the tax collector with great displeasure, began to pray.

3: (Very proudly) God, I am thankful I am not like other men. I am clean and holy. I do everything the Law says I should do. Everyone sees how righteous I am. And they praise me for it. I am not like the robbers, evildoers, or adulterers. (Pointing) And I especially am not like this tax collector. I fast twice a week. I give a tenth of all I get. Isn't that wonderful!

2: While the Pharisee was praying, everyone was impressed. And the more impressed they were, the more the Pharisee prayed. But, no one even took notice of the tax collector. Standing behind the temple pillar, he would not even look up to heaven. He was too humble in God's presence. He just kept beating on his chest and repeating,

4: (Beating on chest, speaking very quietly and humbly) Oh God, I am not a righteous man. But I am a sinner. Please, God, be merciful to me! Please, have mercy on me, a sinner.

2: After they had both finished praying, they left the temple (exit). The Pharisee left still acting very proud, while the tax collector walked out slowly nodding his head, knowing that God had surely heard his prayer and forgiven him.

1: Jesus said,

2: That's just the way it is! Everyone who exalts himself before God will be humbled. But those who humble themselves before God will be exalted.

CURRICULUM FOR INTERGENERATIONAL LEARNING

Unit Title: Celebrating God's Love
Session: 9
Title: The God Who Seeks
Scripture: Luke 15:1-7
Theme: God's love is so great that He goes out to look for those who do not know Him, so they can become His children too.

A. Readiness Activity (As families arrive)

Name Tags. Precut a pattern of a sheep's head from construction paper, one for each participant. As families arrive, instruct each person to color the eyes and nose, glue two or three cotton balls on top of the head, put his or her name on it, and hang it around his or her neck with a piece of yarn.

Materials for Name Tags: Sheep's head pattern precut from construction paper, paper punches, markers, crayons, cotton balls, yarn, scissors, glue, instruction card, sample of completed name tag.

B. Group Time (10–20 minutes)

Welcome. Gather the group together and welcome them to the session. Introduce the session theme by inviting a younger child to come up and stand beside you. Blindfold him, spin him around several times, and tell him to try to find his parents. After a brief attempt, instruct one of his parents to come up and lead him back to his seat before taking off the blindfold. State that this is what it is like to be lost. When we are spiritually lost, it means we don't know God. When we don't know God, He comes and helps us find Him. Today they will hear a Bible story that tells something wonderful God does for people who don't know Him.

Materials for Welcome: Blindfold.

Singing. Sing several songs or choruses.

Materials for Singing: Chorus book.

Scripture Presentation. Present the Parable of the Lost Sheep (Luke 15:1-7) by doing a group story. Have group members cluster at one end of the room, holding their name tags in front of their faces. Select a child to be the lost sheep, and an adult to be the shepherd. Have them act out the story, including sound effects, as the story line directs.

After the presentation, break into family units for the discovery project. State that they will be working on a project to reinforce the truth of the story that God loves each person so much that He goes out to look for us so He can make us part of His family.

Materials for Scripture Presentation: Bible, story script, sheephead name tags, actors.

C. Family Discovery Time (20–30 minutes)

Family Banner. Direct each family to make a simple banner that celebrates the message of the parable. Options for banner backing include felt, burlap, poster board, and large grocery sacks that have been cut open. Grocery sacks can also be used for lettering on the banner.

Materials for Banner: Felt, burlap sheets, poster board, large grocery sacks, yarn, stencils, glue, scissors, markers, crayons, material scraps, other miscellaneous craft items, sample of completed project.

Guided Conversation. As families work encourage them to discuss the question, "Why does God look for us?"

D. Sharing Time (15–20 minutes)

Singing. Call the group back together and sing one or two songs or choruses.

Materials for Singing: Chorus book.

Sharing Projects. Have each family show their banner. Suggestion: Hang the banners in the church for others to see and enjoy. Then return them after two or three weeks.

Discussion Exercise. Do a verse-matching game. Select four or five verses. Write out the first half of each verse in one column on a sheet of newsprint. In the other column scramble the order and write the last half of each verse. As the group matches the verse halves, have children come up and draw a line connecting the two correct halves. Recite each verse together at the completion of the exercise.

Wrap up by stating "God really loves us so much, that He actually goes out to find everyone that doesn't know Him. He doesn't wait for us to come to Him. He comes and finds us. He wants everyone to be one of His sheep!" Challenge the group to become sharers of this Good News with others.

Suggested verses: Psalm 103:8; 136:23; John 10:11; Luke 9:10; Matthew 9:36

Materials for Discussion Exercise: Newsprint sheet with verses in two columns, masking tape, marker

Closing. Sing one more song and close in prayer, thanking God for loving us so much that He would seek after all who do not know His love. Pray that He will help you share that message with others.

Materials for Closing: Chorus book.

E. Family Project

Hang your banner in a prominent place in your home. Talk together about what it means to be part of God's family. Then think of another family you know that needs to become part of God's family too. Pray for them. Begin making arrangements to grow closer to them (e.g., inviting them over for dinner, doing things with them, etc.) so you can eventually share the Good News of God's love with them.

STORY SCRIPT: The Lost Sheep (Luke 15:1-7)
(Group Story)

One day all of the tax collectors and sinners were gathering around to listen to Jesus teach. But the Pharisees and teachers of the Law started complaining, "Look at this man! He talks to all these terrible people. He even eats with them!" So Jesus told them this story.

A shepherd was out in the field with his sheep one day. He looked up into the sky and saw that the sun was starting to go down. So he decided it was time to herd his sheep home. He began counting the sheep to make sure they were all there. The sheep merrily "baa'ed" as the shepherd moved among them to count them.

But as the shepherd was counting, one of the little lambs decided to wander off. When he finished his counting, he scratched his head and thought to himself, "I counted only 99. There are supposed to be 100! Maybe I should count them again." So he did. But there were still only 99. So as the sheep "baa'ed" merrily, the shepherd counted them again. But there were still only 99.

So thinking to himself that the last little lamb must be lost, he left the flock to go look for him. He searched everywhere; behind rocks, in the bushes, next to trees. Finally, he found the little lamb! He was very happy. He threw the little lamb on his shoulders and took him back to the flock.

When the other sheep saw him coming with the little lamb, they rejoiced with the shepherd and "baa'ed" very loudly.

When the sheep were all together, the shepherd went home and called to his friends and neighbors, "Come out and celebrate with me. I have found my little lost lamb." And the flock continued to baa very loudly.

Then Jesus said, "This is just the way it is in heaven when one sinner repents. There is more rejoicing when one sinner repents, than over ninety-nine righteous people who do not need to repent."

CURRICULUM FOR INTERGENERATIONAL LEARNING

Unit Title:	Celebrating God's Love
Session:	10
Title:	The God Who Watches
Scripture:	Luke 15:11-32
Theme:	God's love is so great that when we walk away from Him, He eagerly watches for us to come back, and welcomes us joyfully when we do.

A. Readiness Activity (As families arrive)

Bulletin Board. Letter a heading on a bulletin board "Signs of God's Love." Cut out various street sign shapes from colored construction paper, one for each participant. As families arrive instruct them to write down on each sign one way God shows His loving care in our lives. Have them staple their signs on the bulletin board wherever they choose.

Materials for Bulletin Board: Precut street sign shapes from construction paper, markers, crayons, staplers, staples, instruction card, sample of completed sign.

B. Group Time (10–20 minutes)

Welcome. Gather the group together and welcome them to the session. Introduce the session theme by holding up a dog leash and asking for someone to say what it is. Ask, "What is a dog leash used for?" After several responses say, "Suppose your dog decided to run away. You look and look everywhere for him but cannot find him anywhere. What would you do?" After several responses state that the only real thing you could do in this situation is wait until the dog came home. Today they will be hearing a Bible story about a son who left home, and what his father did about it. It will teach an important lesson about God's love.

Materials for Welcome: Dog leash.

Singing. Sing several songs or choruses.

Materials for Singing: Chorus book.

Scripture Presentation. Present the Parable of the Prodigal Son (Luke 15:11-32) using the overhead projector story, "The Prodigal Son," from Bill Hovey Visuals (see resource listing in back of book).

After the presentation, break into family units for the discovery project. State that they will be working on a project to reinforce the truth from the story that God's love is so great that when we walk away from Him, He eagerly watches for us to come back. And when we do return, He welcomes us joyfully. Give instructions for the discovery activity.

Materials for Scripture Presentation: Bible, overhead projector, story transparencies, projection screen, extension cord, story script.

C. Family Discovery Time (20–30 minutes)

Window of Love. Have a large sheet of poster board for each family, preferably pastel or light colors. Instruct each family to design a stained-glass window using the poster board. Using pictures and lettering from magazines, or artwork, they are to put a special message of God's love in each panel of the window. The intent of this project is to give it away to someone else after the session.

Materials for Window: Poster board, magazines, construction paper, glue, scissors, markers, crayons, sample of completed project.

Guided Conversation. As families work encourage them to discuss to whom they will be giving their projects after the session.

D. Sharing Time (15–20 minutes)

Singing. Call the group back together and sing one or two songs or choruses.

Materials for Singing: Chorus book.

Sharing Projects. Ask families to show their windows and tell to whom they intend to give them.

Discussion Exercise. Bible verse scramble game: Write Psalm 36:5 on a piece of poster board. Cut the verse apart so each word is on a separate card. The reference should also be on a separate card. Tape the verse to a chalkboard, or tack it on a bulletin board, in a scrambled order. Put the cards in the proper order as the group unscrambles the verse. Say the verse together.

Wrap up by saying, "God is just like the father in the story. He eagerly watches and waits for us to come back to Him when we have run away from Him. And when we come back, He welcomes us joyfully. Because He loves us very much, He always watches over us!"

Materials for Discussion Exercise: Bible verse word cards, masking tape or tacks, chalkboard or bulletin board.

Closing. Sing one more song and close in prayer, thanking God for His great love that watches for us and welcomes us when we come to him.

Materials for Closing: Chorus book.

E. Family Project

Talk about the person(s) who will be receiving your Window of Love. Isolate some needs they have for which you can pray as a family. Decide how you will explain to them the meaning of the window and why you want to give it to them. Then make an appointment to visit them.

FAMILIES GROWING TOGETHER

Unit Title:	Celebrating God's Love
Session:	11
Title:	The God Who Trusts
Scripture:	Luke 19:11-27
Theme:	Because of His love God has given each of us different talents with which to serve Him.

A. Readiness Activity (As families arrive)

Door Decoration. On the door to your meeting room, make a scene background of a large tree without leaves on the limbs. On the background above the tree, letter the heading "Our Talent Tree." Precut two or three patterns of leaves from construction paper, one for each participant. As families arrive instruct them to write their names on one side of a leaf. On the other side of the leaf they should write or draw a picture of something they enjoy doing or that they do well. Each one should then punch a hole in the leaf, tie a short piece of yarn through the hole, and tape it to a limb on the tree.

Materials for Door Decoration: Precut leaf patterns from construction paper, markers, crayons, yarn, scissors, Scotch Tape, scene background, instruction card, sample of completed leaf.

B. Group Time (10–20 minutes)

Welcome. Gather the group together and welcome them to the session. Introduce the session theme by inviting several people, both children and adults, to come to the front of the room. Ask them to act out for the group the particular item they drew on their leaf during the readiness activity. Let the rest of the group guess what each one is doing. State that all of these things these individuals have just acted out we call talents. Talents are things that we do well, and/or enjoy doing. Explain that they will be hearing a Bible story today that gives some important information about what we should do with our talents.

Singing. Sing several songs or choruses.

Materials for Singing: Chorus book.

Scripture Presentation. Present the Parable of the Talents using the filmstrip "The Parable of the Talents," from Bible Story Filmstrips (produced by Gospel Light Publications). Have several copies of the script ready and recruit several people to read the parts of the various characters in the story.

After the filmstrip break into family units for the discovery project. State that they will be working on a project to reinforce the truth from the story that God has given us all different talents. Talents are the different things we do well, and enjoy doing. He wants us to use those talents to serve Him. Give instructions for the discovery activity.

Materials for Scripture Presentation: Bible, filmstrip, filmstrip projector, copies of script, projection screen, extension cord.

C. Family Discovery Time (20–30 minutes)

Family Talent Catalog. Using construction paper instruct families to make a book depicting all the talents and abilities each family member has; i.e., things they are good at, things they enjoy doing, etc. Each family member should have his or her own page, with their name showing at the top. They should then use magazine lettering or pictures, or artwork to depict those talents or abilities of each one. Make a cover and bind the book together with yarn.

Materials for Catalog: Construction paper, yarn, scissors, glue, markers, crayons, magazines, paper punches, sample of completed project.

Guided Conversation. As families work on their projects encourage them to discuss the question, "How can we use our talents to serve God?"

D. Sharing Time (15–20 minutes)

Singing. Call the group back together and sing one or two songs or choruses.

Materials for Singing: Chorus book.

Sharing Projects. Ask each family to share their talent catalog with the rest of the group. Each family member should share one talent from his or her own page.

Discussion Exercise. Lead into the discussion exercise by stating that God has given us all many talents. He gave many talents to people in the Bible too. You want to play a game now to discover the many ways people in the Bible used their talents to serve God.

Play "Who's Who?" On a sheet of newsprint, write clues

about a specific talent certain biblical characters had and how they used them for God. Have the group guess who each one is. Write the name of each character next to the clue as each is identified.

Suggested Clues:

● He preached about Jesus all across Asia and Europe. (Paul)

● He used his great strength to free Israel from the Philistines. (Samson)

● He wrote and sang psalms to the Lord. (David)

● She was always doing good and helping the poor. (Dorcas)

● He prayed for rain after a long drought. (Elijah)

● He encouraged others to keep serving Jesus. (Barnabas)

Wrap up by saying, "God's people used their talents to serve God in many ways. Each of us has things we can do and enjoy doing. God has given us those talents. There are many ways we can use them to serve Him. In fact, He gave these abilities to us so we could serve Him better. So don't keep them to yourself. Share them with others. Like money, it always feels better when you spend it!"

Materials for Discussion Exercise: Newsprint sheet with clues written on it, marker, masking tape or tacks, bulletin board or chalkboard.

Closing. Sing a final chorus and close in prayer, thanking God for all the good talents and abilities He has given everyone in your group.

E.Family Project

Talk together about the many talents each family member has that you included in your Family Talent Catalog. Pray and thank God for all the things He has made you able to do. Then have each family member choose one talent and discuss together how that talent can be used during the next week to serve God.

CURRICULUM FOR INTERGENERATIONAL LEARNING

Unit Title: Celebrating God's Love
Session: 12
Title: Planning Session for Service of Celebration
Scripture: Review of previous sessions
Theme: God's love is so great that we as His children should joyfully celebrate it.

A. Readiness Activity (As families arrive)

Mural. Post a large sheet of newsprint on the wall. In large block letters write the word "LOVE." As families arrive instruct them to glue lightly crumpled pieces of colored tissue paper within the outline of the letters. The final effect should be that of a mosaic or stained-glass picture.

Materials for Mural: Newsprint with "LOVE" printed on it, colored sheets of tissue paper, glue, instruction card.

B. Group Time (10–15 minutes)

Welcome. Gather the group together and welcome them to the session. On a premade overhead projector transparency, list all the session themes from the unit. Use this to review briefly the unit theme. Introduce this session by stating that because God's love is so great, we should always celebrate it together as His children. Your session today will focus on a particular way to do just that.

Materials for Welcome: Premade overhead projector transparency, overhead projector, projection screen, extension cord.

Singing. Sing several songs or choruses.

Materials for Singing: Chorus book.

Introduce Planning Session. State that the purpose of this session is for each family unit to work alone or together with one or two other family units to prepare a contribution for a Family Praise Service — session 13. Break into family units or clusters and give instructions for the planning time.

C. Family Discovery Time (20–30 minutes)

Family Planning Time. Distribute the planning guide. In their groups, they should look over the planning guide. Then review together the various session themes as shown on the overhead projector. Each family unit or group should decide how to communicate one or more of these messages, using the suggestions from the planning guide. After 20–30 minutes call for families to write down on a piece of paper what they will be presenting and bring it to you.

Materials for Planning Time: Planning guide, paper, and pencils.

D. Sharing Time (15–20 minutes)

Singing. Call the group back together and sing one or two songs or choruses.

Materials for Singing: Chorus book.

Discussion Exercise. Point to the mural from the readiness activity. Ask the group to give you words beginning with each of the letters from the word "LOVE," that describe God's love for us. Write the words on the mural as each one is said.

Wrap up by saying, "Next week we will be celebrating together the many ways God shows His love to us. We will have a great time together!" Challenge them to practice their contribution to the Service of Celebration. Inform them that when they arrive next session, you will have an order of service listed on an overhead projector transparency and projected on a screen.

Materials for Discussion Exercise: Mural from readiness activity, marker.

Closing. Sing one more song or chorus. Break into family units once again. Instruct them to have a closing prayer time, thanking God for all the ways He shows His love for us. Encourage them to refer to the mural from the Discussion Exercise.

Materials for Closing: Chorus Book.

E. Family Project

Review and practice your contribution for the Family Service of Celebration.

PLANNING GUIDE FOR THE FAMILY SERVICE OF CELEBRATION

SESSION OBJECTIVE:

For each family unit to plan a contribution to the Family Service of Praise, the family praise service which will conclude our time together.

SERVICE COMPONENTS:

1. Prayer—plan a prayer experience to share with the group. Perhaps some type of group response could be a part of this. Or simply writing a prayer to be read would be appropriate.

2. Music—a song, vocal or instrumental, to be presented by your family. Or, lead the group in a special song together.

3. Scripture—a creative presentation of a Scripture passage or passages that relate to our theme throughout the series. Creative forms of presentation are:

- a litany
- choral reading
- two or three different passages woven together in a scripted reading
- antiphonal reading of a single passage
- responsive reading.

The many Scriptures used throughout the series would be good ones to use.

4. A Reading—write and read a modern psalm, a poem, a creative litany or responsive reading.

DIRECTIONS:

1. Decide what you are going to do.

2. Write it down and give it to the session leader so he can make out the order of service.

3. Plan it.

4. Practice it.

5. Pray together as a family that God will prepare you for the service.

Unit Title: Celebrating God's Love
Session: 13
Title: Family Service of Celebration
Scripture: 1 John 3:1-3; Romans 8:31-39

A. BEFORE THE SESSION

1. Before the session, prepare an order of service based on the contributions each family turned in at the previous session. Plan the service with variety in mind, inserting choruses, Scripture readings, and prayer and sharing exercises where necessary.

2. Write the order of service on an overhead transparency and project it on a projection screen so families will see where they will come in the service.

3. Post the "LOVE" mural from last session's Readiness Activity in a conspicuous place in the service area.

4. Prepare a brief meditation about the "Greatness of God's Love" from 1 John 3:1-3 or Romans 8:31-39, and an appropriate closing for your service.

B. DURING THE SESSION

1. Welcome the group to your last session together. State that in this session you will be celebrating together the great love God has shown to us in so many ways. Point the group's attention to the projected overhead transparency. Indicate that each family group should go ahead when it is their turn, without introduction.

2. Proceed with the service of celebration.

3. Wrap up your service with your meditation and the closing you have planned.

4. Be sure to thank your group for their participation in your intergenerational learning series.

OPTIONAL CLOSING SESSION

In the event your series is less than thirteen weeks, and you would like a different kind of closing session, try this option.

Unit Title: Celebrating God's Love
Session: Last Session of Unit
Scripture: 1 John 3:1-3; Romans 8:31-39
Theme: Family Love Feast

A. BEFORE THE SESSION

1. At the end of the previous session, instruct your participants to bring nutritious snack foods to your last session; e.g., cheeses, raw vegetables, fruit, crackers. Your intention is to celebrate the goodness of God's love by sharing together in a love feast and a special family communion service. You will provide the tableware and drinks.

2. Set up your room with a large serving table at one end, with other tables around the room for families to work on poster board banners. You will need enough large sheets of poster board, one for each family, as well as markers and crayons.

3. On an overhead transparency write the various themes from the previous sessions. Project this on a screen so families can see it as they enter the room.

4. Prepare a family communion module for each family. Each module should consist of one common cup of grape juice and a small loaf of bread. Place the communion modules on a separate table.

5. Gather the necessary paper plates, napkins, paper drinking cups, and any serving utensils you will need for your feast. Also prepare a drink to serve.

B. DURING THE SESSION

1. As families arrive instruct them to place their food trays on the serving table, and take their seats at the tables around the room.

2. Open your time with a chorus or two. Distribute the poster board and markers or crayons. Instruct families to make a simple banner representing one of the session themes; refer to the list projected on the screen by the overhead projector.

While they are working, prepare the food to be served.

3. When families are finished, invite them to tape their banners to the fronts of the tables around the room. Then lead the group in a prayer of thanksgiving, after which they are free to serve themselves.

4. After they have finished eating, request that they clean up their tables, and that each family pick up a communion module from the table. Invite them to sit as families on the floor or around the tables as you share together in communion.

5. Conduct a communion service.

6. Close by joining together in a large circle and singing the Doxology.

A NINE-SESSION INTERGENERATIONAL LEARNING PROGRAM

Unit Title:	A Great God Who Does Great Things
Scripture Focus:	Jesus' Miracles from the Gospel of Mark
Unit Theme:	The Miracles of Jesus powerfully demonstrate the caring touch of the Lord in the midst of human need and difficulty. Jesus brought hope, grace, and deliverance into the lives of hurting people. This learning unit is designed to lead participants in exploring the many ways God reaches out and touches our lives with His love and care.

1. He Gives Courage in Faith (Mark 2:1-12)
Theme

The four men believed Jesus could heal their friend. That faith gave them courage to bring him to Jesus to be healed.

Readiness Activity

Name Tags—on a half sheet of construction paper write your first name, and draw a picture of something you do to help at home. Hang it around your neck with a piece of yarn and share it with others.

Scripture Presentation

Simultaneous mime

Family Discovery Time

Friendship Cards—Using construction paper, artwork, magazine pictures, Scripture verses, etc., make one or more greeting cards with a message of hope and encouragement. Decide to whom each card will be given or sent. Be sure to follow up by mailing the cards later.

Discussion Exercise

Verse Scramble using Galatians 6:9

2. He Brings Peace in Difficulty (Mark 4:35-41)

Theme

Jesus brought peace to the disciples in a life-threatening storm.

Readiness Activity

Using pipe cleaners and different colored facial tissues, make a small bouquet of flowers. Put them in a Styrofoam cup. After the session, deliver your flowers to someone with whom you would like to share some cheer.

Scripture Presentation

Group Story—have one person play Jesus, several play disciples, and divide the group up into the various elements of the storm (i.e., wind, rain, waves, thunder).

Family Discovery Time

Praise Block—Make a large block out of poster board. On each side of the block put magazine pictures, artwork, or Scripture verses representing ways God helps us in difficult times. Option: Include pictures representing a time God specifically helped you during a difficult experience.

Discussion Exercise

Picture Identification Game—On pieces of poster board mount several pictures of people experiencing problems. Have the group identify, "How can Jesus help these people with their problems?"

3. He Supplies Our Need (Mark 6:30-44)

Theme

Jesus is able to supply all our needs, just as He fed the hungry crowd.

Readiness Activity

Bulletin Board—Post a large picture of an umbrella with the words lettered on it "Showers of Blessing." Each one should write or draw ways God blesses us on raindrop-shaped cutouts and staple them to the bulletin board.

Scripture Presentation

Filmstrip

Suggested Resource: "Jesus Feeds 5,000," from Bible Story Filmstrips (Gospel Light Publications)

Family Discovery Time

Collage—On poster board make a collage demonstrating ways God provides for our needs using words and pictures from magazines. Frame it with construction-paper strips.

Discussion Exercise

Ball of String Sharing Game—Form a large circle. One person holds large ball of string. That person shares something he or she is thankful that God supplies. Holding on to string they toss the ball to someone else letting the string unwind. The person catching the ball then shares in the same way. This continues until almost everyone has had a chance to share.

4. He Touches the Untouchable (Mark 7:24-30)

Theme

Jesus broke down all social/racial barriers by healing the daughter of a woman considered untouchable by His friends.

Readiness Activity

"God Loves _____" Badges—Write "God Loves _____" on circle-shaped cutouts. Tape a safety pin to the back of the cutout. Give it to someone else in the room, filling in that person's name on the blank line.

Scripture Presentation

Skit

Family Discovery Time

Hands That Reach Mobile—Trace and cut out hands of each family member. On one side of hand cutout, glue magazine pictures, use artwork, or write words or Bible verses expressing ways you can reach out to others with the Good News of Jesus Christ. On the other side of the cutout, draw or glue pictures of people in our world that are ignored, neglected, or shunned. Use yarn to hang the cutouts from a wire clothes hanger or wood dowel rod.

Discussion Exercise

Bible Rebus—make one or more Bible rebuses and discuss the meaning of each verse as it is guessed. Suggested verses: Exodus 33:14; Psalm 46:1; Psalm 91:1-2; Matthew 11:28-29.

5. He Feels Our Hurt (Mark 5:21-43)

Theme

When Jesus raised Jairus' daughter from the dead, He not only healed her, but He healed the deep hurt Jairus felt over the loss of his daughter.

Readiness Activity

Bookmark—Make a "God Cares for You" bookmark from a construction-paper strip. Color and decorate it. Then trade with someone else in the group.

Scripture Presentation

Filmstrip

Suggested Resource: "The Little Sleeping Beauty," Arch Filmstrips on Video (Concordia Publishing House)

Family Discovery Time

Book of Encouragement—Using construction paper, markers, crayons, magazine pictures and yarn, make a book with a message of encouragement and hope for someone with whom you would like to share God's love. Discuss to whom you will give your book when it's finished.

Discussion Exercise

Alphabet Game—Write the alphabet on a sheet of butcher paper. Have group members give one-word answers beginning with each letter of the alphabet in answer to the question, "How can we touch other people's hurts like Jesus did?"

6. He Gives Light in Darkness (Mark 10:46-52)

Theme

The blind man lived in darkness until Jesus brought light into his world by healing him.

Readiness Activity

Door Decoration—Cover the door with navy-blue construction paper. Letter a heading that says "Jesus Lights Up My Night." Post a large, bright-yellow light bulb in the middle of the door. Each one should write his or her name on a strip of yellow construction paper and tape it on the door as a ray of light coming from the bulb.

Scripture Presentation
Puppet Drama
Suggested Resources: Arch Book and cassette "Jesus and Bartimaeus"; "Stories of Jesus" cassette #5 from the *Stories That Live* series, book 5.

Family Discovery Time
Sports Pennant—Make a sports pennant that proclaims the message of the story.

Discussion Exercise
Picture Puzzle—Make a large collage of several pictures of people reaching out to help someone in need. Cut it apart in various shapes. Scramble shapes and tape to chalkboard. Reassemble puzzle as a large group. Invite children to come up and put pieces in right place. Discuss what the picture says about the many ways we can bring the light of Christ into the lives of others.

7. He Does What No One Else Can Do (Mark 9:14-29)

Theme
Jesus alone had the power to bring deliverance to the demon-possessed boy.

Readiness Activity
Post a large picture of the symbol from Arm and Hammer Baking Soda in the middle of the bulletin board. Letter one of these headings: "Christ Strengthens Me," "Greater Is He," "Jesus, the Strength Within." Each one should trace and cut out a hammer from construction paper, put their name on it, and staple it to the bulletin board.

Scripture Presentation
Overhead Projector Presentation
Story Script Resource: *Stories of Jesus, Stories of Now*, by Alex Campbell (Walnut, Calif.: Educational Ministries, Inc.)

Family Discovery Time
Patchwork Quilt—Make a group patchwork quilt. Have each

family make two or three panels from large sheets of construction paper. Using artwork, pictures from magazines, and Scripture verses, each panel should display something Jesus can do for us that no one else can. Tape the squares together and hang in the church for others to enjoy.

Discussion Exercise

Coded Verse Game Suggested Verses: Psalm 116:7; John 16:33b; Philippians 4:13.

8. Planning Session for the Family Praise Service

Readiness Activity

"Praise" Mosaic — Tear different colors of construction paper into small pieces of various shapes. Write the word "PRAISE" in large block letters on a newsprint sheet. Glue paper pieces within the outline of the letters.

Scripture Presentation

Review the unit theme by reviewing story themes from previous sessions. Focus on the great things God does for us because He is such a great God.

Family Discovery Time

Modern Psalm — Have each family write a modern psalm of praise for all the great things God has done for them. They will each read their psalm at the Family Praise Service (session 9).

Discussion Exercise

Graffiti — Ask group to offer one word or short phrases in answer to the question, "How can we praise God for all the great things He does for us?" Write the answer on the mural from the Readiness Activity.

9. Family Service of Praise

Plan a Family Praise Service, featuring group singing and the modern psalms families have written. Prepare a closing meditation from Psalm 107 or Psalm 111.

10. Alternate Final Sessions

If you desire to run a series of eight sessions or less, try using the Love Feast option suggested in the previous unit. Or, session eight above can easily be modified to be a fitting concluding session for this unit.

A NINE-SESSION PARENT-TEEN LEARNING UNIT

One of the strengths of intergenerational learning is the opportunity to draw parents and teens in the church together for a time of interaction in a nonthreatening environment. The informality of intergenerational learning facilitates communication between parents and teens without forcing issues. It also helps alleviate the sense of awkwardness that can sometimes accompany parent-teen dialogue. The freedom of expression involved in intergenerational learning helps create an open atmosphere where parents and teens can learn biblical truths while they learn about themselves and each other.

The following suggested unit is based on the Fruit of the Spirit, as expressed in Galatians 5:22-25. The Fruit of the Spirit passage offers a simple outline for building an extended learning unit.

Unit Title: Taste the Fruit
Scripture Focus: Fruit of the Spirit in Galatians 5:16-25.

> **Unit Theme:** The Holy Spirit is our key to living a Christlike life. He ministers to us to mold and transform us into the image of Christ. Therefore, we are called to keep in step with the Spirit, and demonstrate the qualities of Christ in our lives. These qualities are called the Fruit of the Spirit. This unit is designed to help participants better understand and apply the Fruit of the Spirit to daily living in Jesus Christ.

1. *Scripture Focus:* For your Scripture Focus for each session, refer to the InterVarsity Press Bible study guide, *The Fruit of the Spirit,* by Hazel Offner (I.V.P., 1977). This will provide ample Scripture texts for establishing your focus for each session.

2. *Scripture Presentation.* In working with parents and teens, the options for story presentation are much the same as for any other type of intergenerational group. One additional option is the approach of reading a selected passage and asking some basic information-and-application questions. You can also use choral, group, or responsive reading techniques. If your Scripture passage is narrative rather than story oriented, after reading the passage, engage the group in a word substitution exercise. That is, isolate key words and phrases and ask the group to substitute other words that help define the isolated terms. These approaches can be used quite effectively when varied with other types of presentations.

3. *Learning Activities.* Here are two options you can use.

Option One: Provide a large piece of felt, or other type of material for each family to make a banner. Instruct them to divide their material into nine sections. Each week, they will fill in a section of their banner with words, symbols, or other artwork to coincide with the particular "fruit" studied that session (i.e., love, joy, peace). At the end of the series each family will then have a single banner they can hang somewhere in their home.

Option Two: Use any of the following suggested activities in your sessions. You can use three to five in a single session as learning centers. In this case families would be divided into clusters at specific work centers, according to their choice. Or, they can work as individual family units at various activity centers. In succeeding sessions, vary the activities, offering them in different combinations. Another option is to use one activity per session, letting individual family units complete their own project, or work with another family unit.

a. Advertising Brochure. Make a trifold advertising brochure, announcing the sale of a particular Fruit of the Spirit.

b. Bumper Stickers. Using colored Con-Tact paper, make bumper stickers focusing on a specific message about a particular Fruit of the Spirit. Decide as a family to whom you can give your sticker(s) to share with them about the Fruit of the Spirit.

c. Banner. On burlap, felt, or a large grocery sack that has been split open, make a banner which proclaims the meaning and application of one of the Fruits of the Spirit. Hang banners in the church for the congregation to enjoy.

d. Collage. Creatively illustrate one of the Fruits of the Spirit by making a collage on poster board, using magazine pictures and lettering.

e. Commercial. Write a commercial advertising one of the Spirit's Fruits. Use both music and dialogue. Record your commercials on cassette tape and play them during the announcement time in successive Sunday worship services (i.e., one commercial each service).

f. Creative Definitions. Write a creative piece about one of the Spirit's Fruits, defining it in terms of concrete action. For example, "The Fruit of the Spirit is patience with . . . when. . . ."

g. Crossword Game. Make a crossword game to share with the rest of the group. Focus on a particular Fruit of the Spirit.

h. Drama. Depict a Fruit of the Spirit in action, or a situation where a particular Fruit is lacking.

i. Employment Ad. Write an employment ad, advertising the need for a person who practices a certain Fruit of the Spirit. Include such things as salary, benefits, qualifications, job description, etc.

j. Fruit Mobile. Make a mobile which illustrates one of the Spirit's Fruit in action.

k. Media Presentation. Write a story depicting two characters, one who demonstrates one of the Spirit's Fruits and one who does not. Draw illustrations on write-on slides, a filmstrip, or overhead transparencies. Record your story script on a cassette tape to play when you present your story to the group.

l. Picture Pyramid. Make a large pyramid out of poster board. Cut out magazine pictures and lettering to creatively illustrate one of the Spirit's Fruits. Glue them to the pyramid. Set the pyramid on a coffee table at home to share with others.

m. Puppet Show. Make and use finger, stick, sack, or sock puppets to present a creative drama illustrating one of the Spirit's Fruits.

n. Rebus. Using a Bible concordance, select a verse relating to one of the Spirit's Fruits. Make a rebus of that verse to share with the rest of the group.

o. Wanted Poster. Make a wanted poster announcing the "danger" of a person wanted for demonstrating a particular Fruit of the Spirit. Include both a picture of the wanted person and script.

4. *Discussion Exercises.* Having a group of teens and parents gives the added advantage of broadening the possible discussion activities you can use. In addition to those used in the preceding learning units, the resources listed in the back of the book will provide many possible activities to reinforce learning. Also, many of the activities listed above will provide built-in opportunities for discussion activity without planning for an extra exercise.

RESOURCES FOR INTERGENERATIONAL PROGRAMMING

A. SOURCES GIVING A CONCEPTUAL FRAMEWORK AND HELPS FOR ORGANIZING INTERGENERATIONAL MINISTRIES IN THE CHURCH

Harder, Bertha and Marlene Kropf. *Intergenerational Learning in the Church* (Newton, Kan.: Faith and Life Press, 1982).

Money, Royce. *Building Stronger Families: Family Enrichment in the Home, Church and Community* (Wheaton, Ill.: Victor Books, 1984).

Sawin, Margaret M. *Family Enrichment with Family Clusters* (Valley Forge, Pa.: Judson Press, 1979).

Sell, Charles M. *Family Ministry: The Enrichment of Family Life Through the Church* (Grand Rapids, Mich.: Zondervan Publishers, 1981).

White, James W. *Intergenerational Religious Education* (Birmingham, Ala.: Religious Education Press, 1988).

B. LEARNING RESOURCES DESIGNED SPECIFICALLY

FOR FAMILY AND INTERGENERATIONAL PRO-
GRAMMING FOR THE CHURCH, WITH BOTH BIBLI-
CAL AND TOPICAL THEMES

Davis, Mary Jane. "Worship: A Family Affair." Packet of materials for five sessions. Available upon request from Mary Jane
Davis, Grantham Church, Grantham, PA 17027.

Dregni, Meredith Sommers. *Experiencing More with Less*
(Scottdale, Pa.: Herald Press, 1983). Based on the book *Living
More with Less,* provides complete curriculum for five days of
programming in a retreat or camp setting. Adaptable to other
settings.

Gorman, Cinda. *Growing Up Christian in a Sexy World* (Brea,
Calif.: Educational Ministries, Inc.) Six sessions for children
(grades five and six) and their parents, focusing on preparation for adolescence.

Leonard, Joe E. ed. *Church and Family Gatherings* (Valley Forge,
Pa.: Judson Press, 1978). Six units of study, from three to
nine sessions, with complete plans for content and activities.

McGinnis, James. *Helping Families Care: Practical Ideas for Intergenerational Programs* (Bloomington, Ind.: Meyer-Stone
Books, 1989). A variety of programs, strategies and activities
for teaching peace and social justice in intergenerational
settings.

Parents' and Teens' brochure series: "Parents, Your Teenagers
Need You," "The Teenager and His Crowd," "I'm Not Going
to Church Today!" "Can We Treat Children Like People?"
"You Never Trust Me," "What About the Generation Gap?"
"What to Do About Teenage Rebellion," "Can I Have the
Car Tonight?" "I Don't Know What I Want to Be!" "How to
Live With Your Teenager and Like It," "A License to Prac-
tice Family Living," "What Christian Kids Don't Tell Their
Parents." Published and distributed by Christian Ed. Publish-
ers, P.O. Box 261129, San Diego, CA 92126. This series of
brochures is designed for discussion sessions in a parent-teen
context.

Rogers, Jack and Sharee. *The Family Together: Intergenerational
Education in the Church School* (Pasadena, Calif.: Fuller Theo-
logical Society). Outlines themes for fifty-two Sundays from
September through August.

Rupp, Anne Neufeld. *The Family Car* (Brea, Calif.: Educational Ministries, Inc., 1986). Designed for a weekend family camp, consisting of complete plans for four sessions. Adaptable to other settings.

Stowe, Robert. *The Love Feast* (Brea, Calif.: Educational Ministries, Inc., 1987). A two-day, four-session intergenerational retreat focusing on the agape feast of the early church.

Sullender, R. Scott. *Family Enrichment Workshops* (Brea, Calif.: Educational Ministries, Inc., 1982). An eight-session curriculum on family life designed for families with adolescents.

Sunday Festivals Series: "A Covenant With God's People," "Celebrating God's Presence," "The Prophet's Words and Actions," "Be the Good News," "Celebrating God's Good Earth," and "The Drama for the Church at Worship." (Brea, Calif.: Educational Ministries, Inc.) A series of six, individual festival celebrations, each including resources for intergenerational involvement in worship and learning settings.

VanderHaar, Del and Trudy. *Celebrating Thanksgiving* (Orange City, Iowa: Reformed Church in America, 1976). Booklet outlining two models for a family-cluster Thanksgiving celebration. Available from Reformed Church in America, Distribution Center, 3000 Ivanrest SW, Grandville, MI 49418.

VanderHaar, Trudy. *Generations Learning Together in the Congregation* (Orange City, Iowa: Reformed Church in America, 1976). Booklet offering suggestions for various types of intergenerational learning experiences. Available from Reformed Church in America, Distribution Center, 3000 Ivanrest SW, Grandville, MI 49418.

Weaver, Judy. *Celebrating Holidays and Holy Days in Church and Family Settings* (Nashville, Tenn.: Discipleship Resources, 1989). A book of ideas, crafts, games, and recipes for celebrating major Jewish and Christian holy days.

Word Study Packets series: Discipleship, Spirit, Faith, Peace, Hope, Salvation, Promise, Joy, Covenant, Sacrifice, Forgiveness, Obedience, Grace, Freedom, and Power (Durham, N.C.: National Teacher Education Program). A series of studies designed for Advent, Lent, Pentecost, and other times. Each packet contains complete plans for content and activities.

C. SOURCES DESIGNED FOR HOME-FAMILY EXPERIENCES BUT WHICH PROVIDE IDEAS FOR FAMILY AND INTERGENERATIONAL LEARNING EXPERIENCES IN A CHURCH GROUP SETTING

Cooley, Vivien. *Time for Snails and Painting Whales* (Chicago: Moody Press, 1987).

Dellinger, Annette E. *Happy Talk: Devotions for Families with Young Children* (St. Louis, Mo.: Concordia Publishing, 1982).

Dellinger, Annette E. *More Happy Talk* (St. Louis, Mo.: Concordia Publishing, 1982).

Dobson, James. *Preparing for Adolescence, Multi-media Growth Pak* (Distributed by the Educational Products Division of Word, Inc., Waco, Texas).

Hall, Terry. *Finally, Family Devotions That Work* (Chicago: Moody Press, 1986).

Hibbard, Ann. *Family Celebrations: Meeting Christ in Your Holidays and Special Occasions* (Brentwood, Tenn.: Wolgemuth & Hyatt, Publishers, Inc., 1988).

Gaither, Gloria and Shirley Dobson. *Let's Make a Memory* (Waco, Texas: Word Books, 1983).

Krueger, Caryl Waller. *1001 Things to Do with Your Kids* (Nashville, Tenn.: Abingdon Press, 1988).

D. SOURCES PROVIDING CREATIVE LEARNING ACTIVITY IDEAS FOR GENERAL CHRISTIAN EDUCATION EXPERIENCES WHICH CAN BE APPLIED TO FAMILY AND INTERGENERATIONAL SETTINGS

Bolton, Barbara J. *How to Do Bible Learning Activities, Grades 1–6, Vol 2.* (Ventura, Calif.: International Center for Learning, 1984).

Britton, Colleen. *Palestine 30 A.D.: You Are There* (Brea, Calif.: Educational Ministries, Inc., 1987).

Bundschuh, Rich and Annette Parish. *How to do Bible Learning Activities, Grades 7–12, Vol. 2.* (Ventura, Calif.: International Center for Learning, 1984).

Campbell, Alexander. *Heroes Then, Heroes Now* (Brea, Calif.: Educational Ministries, Inc., 1981).

Campbell, Alexander. *Stories of Jesus, Stories of Now* (Brea, Calif.: Educational Ministries, Inc., 1980).

Church Educator magazine, monthly publication. Educational Ministries, Inc., 2861-C Saturn St., Brea, Calif. 92621.

Church Teacher magazine, bimonthly publication. NTEP, 2504 N. Roboro St., Durham, NC 27704.

Daniel, Rebecca. *Jesus: His Parables* (Carthage, Ill.: Shining Star Publications, 1984).

Darkes, Anna Sue. *Projectable Object Lessons* (Lititz, Pa.: Faith Venture Visuals, Inc., 1981).

Davidson, Robert G. *Biblical Arts Festival* (Brea, Calif.: Educational Ministries, Inc., 1988).

Dorsett, Judy. *Handbook of Creativity* (Cincinnati, Ohio: Standard Publishing, 1984).

Gillespie, Rachel Lee. *Learning Centers for Better Christian Education* (Valley Forge, Pa.: Judson Press, 1982).

Goetz, Betty and Ruth Bomberger. *Market Place — 29 A.D.* (Stevensville, Mich.: B. J. Goetz Publishing Co., 1989).

Griffhorn, Thelma. *Things for Kids to Do* (Wheaton, IL: Victor Books, n.d.).

Griggs, Donald. *20 New Ways of Teaching the Bible* (Nashville, Tenn.: Abingdon Press, 1977).

Griggs, Patricia. *Creative Activities in Church Education* (Nashville, Tenn.: Abingdon Press, 1974).

Huitsing, Betty et al. *Adventures in Creative Teaching* (Wheaton, Ill.: Victor Books, 1986).

The Idea Book (Elgin, Ill.: D.C. Cook, 1987).

Klein, Karen. *How to Do Bible Learning Activities, Ages 2–5* (Ventura, Calif.: International Center for Learning, 1982).

Maschke, Ruby A., Abingdon Bible Activities Series: *The Life of Jesus, The Miracles of Jesus, The Parables of Jesus, The Followers of Jesus* (Nashville, Tenn.: Abingdon Press, 1979).

Rodin, Shelly. *When Puppets Talk, People Listen* (Wheaton, Ill.: Scripture Press, n.d.).

Rottman, Fran. *Easy-to-Make Puppets and How to Use Them* (Ventura, Calif.: Regal Books, 1978).

Shining Star magazine, quarterly publication. Shining Star Publications, Box 299, Carthage, Ill. 62321

Smith, Judy Gattis. *Teaching Children about Prayer* (Brea, Calif.: Educational Ministries, Inc., 1988).

Sorlien, Sandra. *Bulletin Boards That Teach* (Minneapolis, Minn.: Augsburg Fortress, 1989).

Stewart, Ed and Neal McBride. *How to Do Bible Learning Activities, Adults* (Ventura, Calif.: International Center for Learning, 1982).

Stewart, Ed and Neal McBride. *How to Do Bible Learning Activities, Grades 7–12, Vol. 1* (Ventura, Calif.: International Center for Learning, 1982).

Stringer, Leslea and Lea Brown. *Craft Handbook for Children's Church* (Grand Rapids, Mich.: Baker Book House, 1981).

Suede-Graph and Super Suede-Graph story sets for the Old and New Testaments (Wheaton, Ill.: Scripture Press).

32 Bible Based Bulletin Boards series, *Volumes 1–4* (Wheaton, Ill.: Scripture Press Publications).

Von Trutzschler, E. G. *Outrageous Object Lessons* (Ventura, Calif.: Gospel Light Publications, 1987).

Vos Wezeman, Phyllis and Colleen Aalsburg Wiessner. *Celebrate: A Creative Approach to Bible Study,* sets 1 and 2. (Brea, Calif.: Educational Ministries, Inc.)

Ward, Elaine. *All about Teaching Peace* (Brea, Calif.: Educational Ministries, Inc., 1989).

Ward, Elaine. *Gifts of the Spirit* (Brea, Calif.: Educational Ministries, Inc., 1988).

Ward, Elaine. *Growing with the Bible* (Brea, Calif.: Educational Ministries, Inc., 1986).

Ward, Elaine. *More Old Testament Stories* (Brea, Calif.: Educational Ministries, Inc., 1984).

Ward, Elaine. *New Testament Stories* (Brea, Calif.: Educational Ministries, Inc., 1984).

Ward, Elaine. *Old Testament Stories* (Brea, Calif.: Educational Ministries, Inc., 1984).

Ward, Elaine. *Using God's Word in Christian Education* (Brea, Calif.: Educational Ministries, Inc., 1987).

E. SOURCES OF MUSIC RECOMMENDED FOR FAMILY AND INTERGENERATIONAL SETTINGS

Lift Him Up chorus books, nos. 1–5. Nashville, Tenn.: The Benson Company.

Praise, Maranatha! chorus book. Distributed by Word, Waco, Texas.

Praise and Worship Songbook, nos. 1–3. Mobile, Ala.: Integrity Music, Inc.

Sunday School Sing-A-Long, cassette tape series. Produced by Maranatha! Music. Distributed by Word, Waco, Texas.

Worship Him chorus books, nos. 1–2. Tempo Music Publications. Distributed by Alexandria House, Alexandria, Ind. Sing-along cassettes also available.

F. SOURCES FOR AUDIOVISUAL MATERIALS

1. FILMSTRIPS

Bible Story Filmstrips, produced by Gospel Light Publications. P. O. Box 6309, Oxnard, CA 93031

Arch Filmstrips on Video, produced by Concordia Publishing House, St. Louis, Mo.

2. BIBLE STORIES ON CASSETTE TAPE

Arch Books Aloud, produced by Concordia Publishing House, St. Louis, Mo.

Stories That Live and *Stories to Remember,* created by Peter Enns. Distributed by Stories That Live, Inc., Tulsa, Okla.

Children's Tape Series, produced by Hosanna Ministries, 2421 Aztec Rd. NE, Albuquerque, NM 87107

The Treasure Chest, produced by Christian Publications, Inc., 1710 Lee Road, Orlando, FL 32810

You Are There series, produced by Scripture Press Publications, Wheaton, Ill.

Suede-Graphs Cassettes, produced by Scripture Press Publications, Wheaton, Ill.

3. EQUIPMENT, SUPPLIES, TEACHING AND STORY TRANSPARENCY SETS FOR THE OVERHEAD PROJECTOR

Bill Hovey Visuals, 5730 Duluth St., Minneapolis, MN 55422

Faith Venture Visuals, 510 E. Main St., P.O. Box 423, Lititz, PA 17543

Scripture Press Publications, 1825 College Ave., Wheaton, IL. 60187.

4. WRITE ON SLIDES/FILMSTRIPS

Ed. Tech. Service Co., P.O. Box 409, Chatham, NJ 07928

The Film Makers, P.O. Box 593, Arcadia, CA 91006

"U" Film, Hudson Photographic Industries, Irvington-On-Hudson, NY 10533

G. THE FOLLOWING RESOURCES ARE CURRENTLY OUT OF PRINT, BUT OFFER VALUABLE HELPS FOR UNDERSTANDING AND ORGANIZING PROGRAMS FOR INTERGENERATIONAL LEARNING IN THE CHURCH

Collins, Gary. *Facing the Future* (Waco, Texas: Word Books, 1976).

Griggs, Donald and Patricia. *Generations Learning Together* (Nashville, Tenn.: Abingdon, 1976). Provides basic information on the why's and how's of intergenerational learning, plus nine units of study.

Harder, Bertha Fast. *Celebrate!* (Newton, Kan.: Faith and Life Press, 1980). Contains ideas for intergenerational celebration of Advent/Christmas and Lent/Easter. Several complete plans for worship services are provided.

Hendrix, Lela. *Extended Family: Combining Ages in Church Experience* (Nashville, Tenn.: Broadman Press, 1979).

Koehler, George E. *Learning Together: A Guide for Intergenerational Education in the Church* (Nashville, Tenn.: Discipleship Resources, 1977).

Larson, Jim and Jill. *Celebrating Togetherness: A Resource Guide for Enriching Family Relationships Through the Church* (Chicago: The Evangelical Covenant Church of America, 1973). Offers a variety of program plans for parent groups, family clusters, couples, family camping, and parent-teen groups.

Larson, Jim and Jill. *To Understand Each Other: A Resource Guide for Family Ministries* (Chicago: The Evangelical Covenant Church of America, 1973). Similar to the previous work, a manual offering a sampling of strategies for family-intergenerational involvement in various formats.

Nutting, Ted R. *Family Cluster Programs: Resources for Intergenerational Bible Study* (Valley Forge, Pa.: Judson Press, 1977). Programs based on the parables, focusing on relationships.

DATE D'